ONE-MEASURE ROCK BEATS
(The Snare on Two and Four)

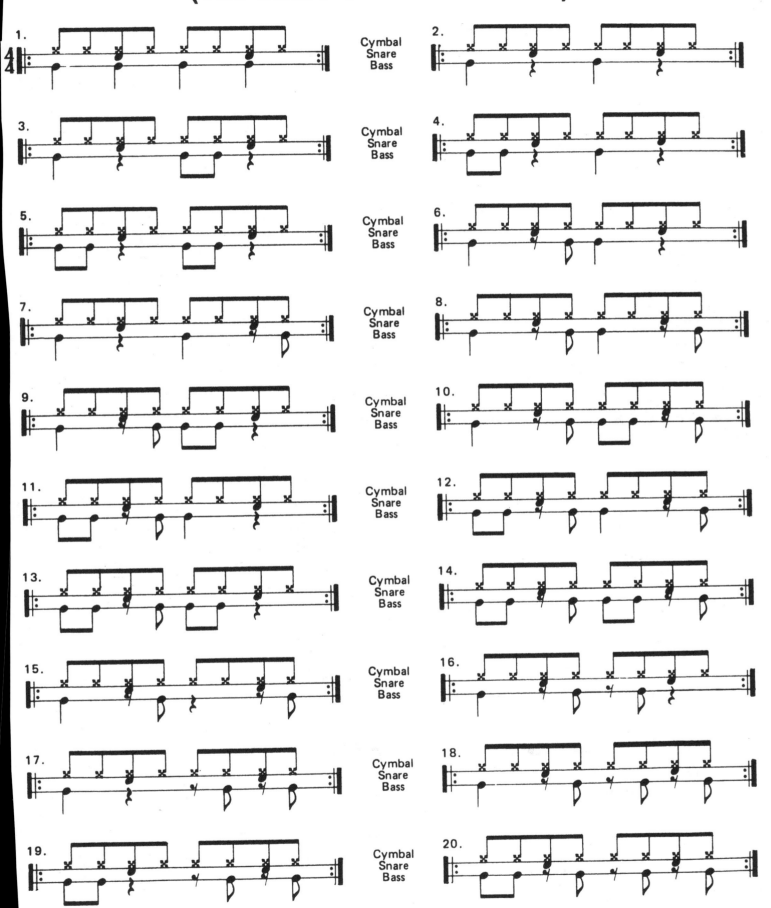

1

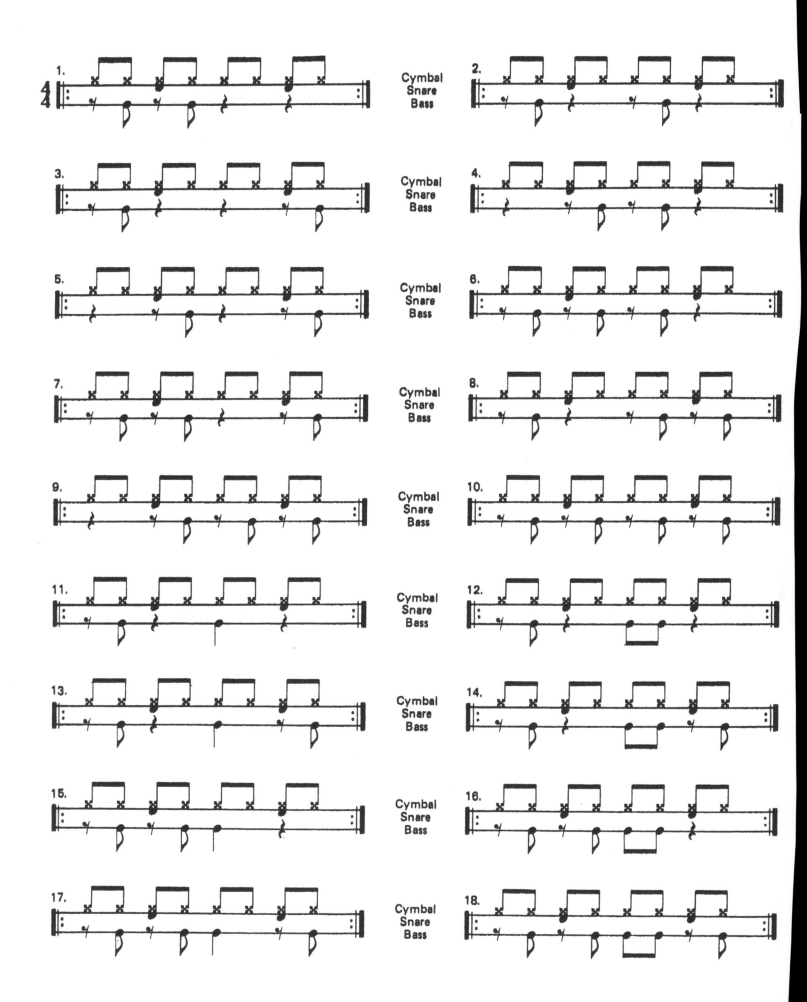

2

TWO-MEASURE COMBINATIONS

1/8 NOTE VARIATIONS FOR SNARE DRUM

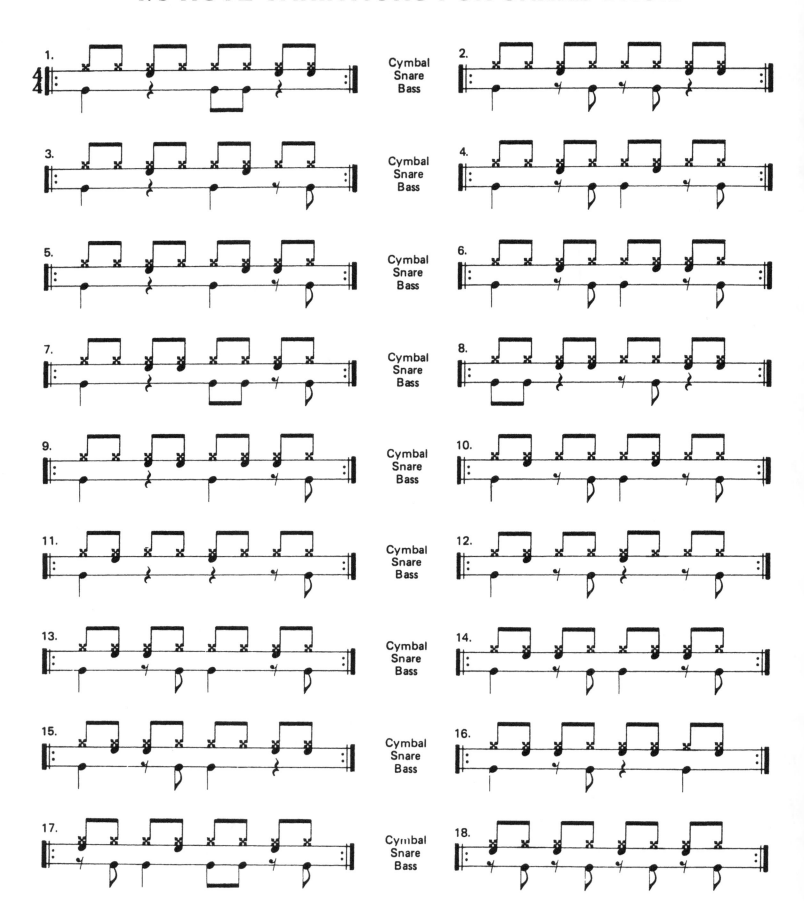

4

1/16 NOTE VARIATIONS FOR SNARE DRUM
(Bass Drum Part Omitted)

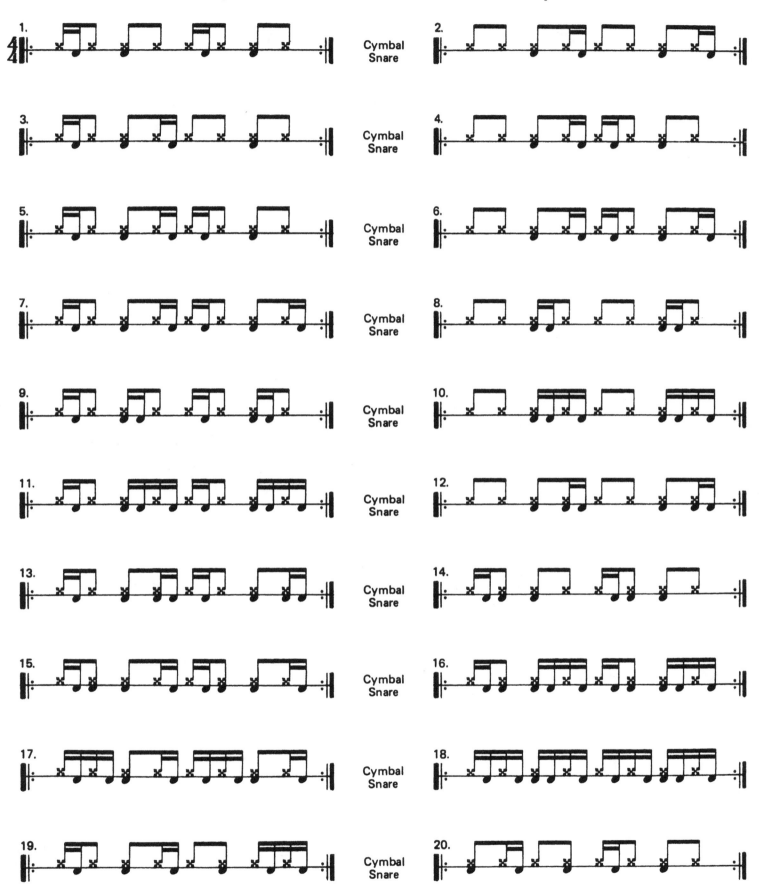

1/16 NOTE VARIATIONS FOR SNARE DRUM
(Bass Drum Part Included)

Cymbal
Snare
Bass

7

1/16 NOTE PATTERNS FOR BASS DRUM – IN 2/4 TIME
(Snare Drum Played on the Count of Two)

1/16 NOTE PATTERNS FOR BASS DRUM – IN 4/4 TIME
(Snare Drum Played on the Count of Two and Four)

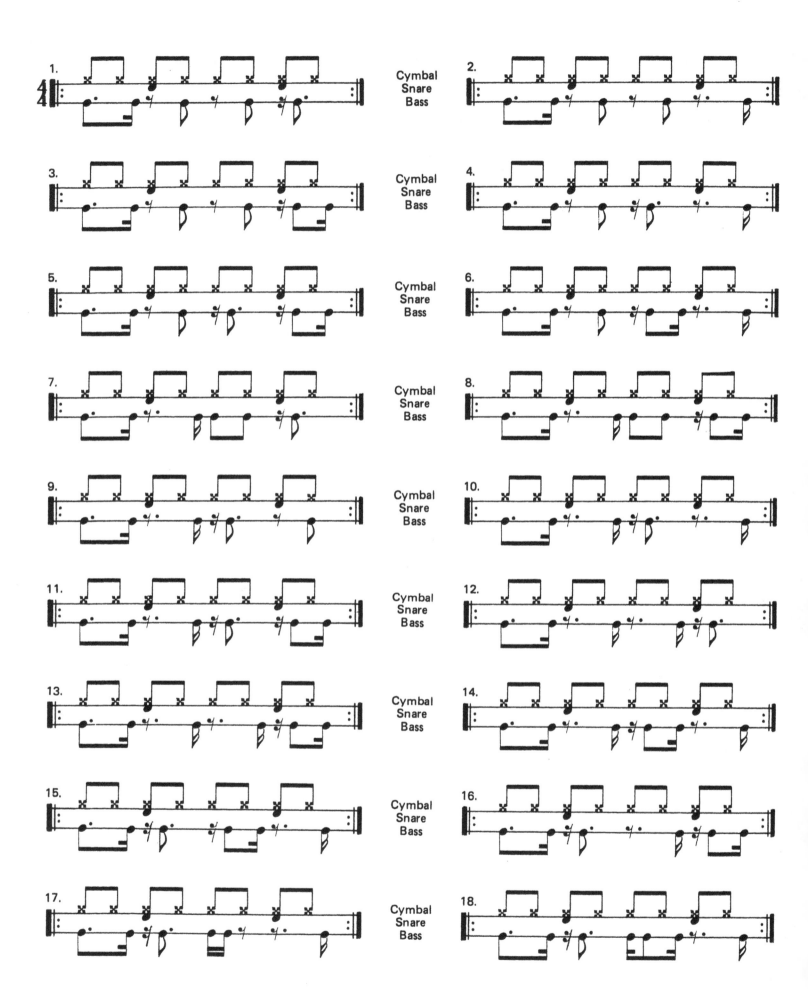

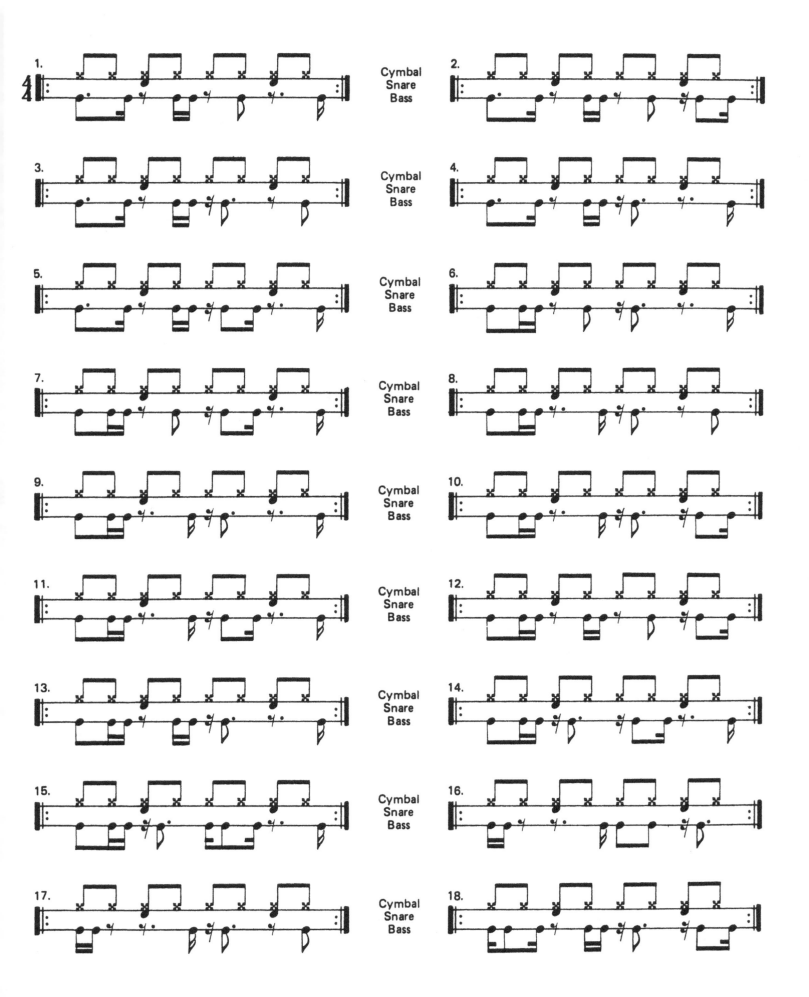

1/16 NOTE PATTERNS FOR BOTH SNARE AND BASS
(IN 2/4 TIME)

13

1/16 NOTE PATTERNS FOR BOTH SNARE AND BASS
(IN 4/4 TIME)

Cymbal
Snare
Bass

1/16 NOTE TRIPLET PATTERNS FOR SNARE DRUM

Precede each exercise with 1½ bars of an ad-lib rock rhythm.

1/16 NOTE TRIPLET PATTERNS
FOR SNARE AND BASS

17

PARTS OF 1/16 NOTE TRIPLETS
BETWEEN THE SNARE AND BASS

32ND NOTE DRAG PATTERNS FOR SNARE

VARIATIONS FOR THE ROCK BEAT
WITH SINGLE PARADIDDLES

A single paradiddle consists of two alternating strokes and a double stroke —— the *para* is the alternating strokes, and the *diddle* is the double stroke.

SAY IT AS YOU PLAY IT

THERE ARE FOUR BASIC SINGLE PARADIDDLES.

In order to bring some variation to playing basic rock time you can simply divide the single paradiddles between the cymbal and snare. Play the right hand part of the paradiddles on the cymbal, and the left hand part on the snare.

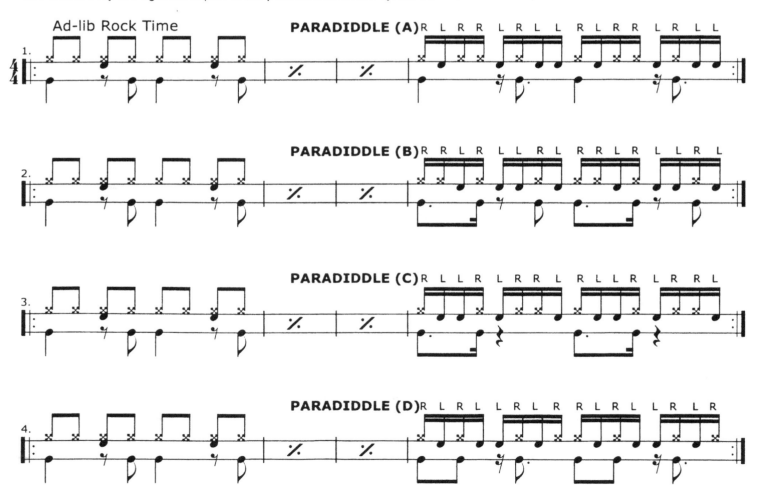

VARIATIONS WITH COMBINATIONS
OF SINGLE PARADDIDLES

SPLITTING SINGLE PARADIDDLES
BETWEEN THE SNARE AND BASS
IN COORDINATION WITH BASIC ROCK TIME

Important: The right-hand part now represents the bass drum, while the left-hand part is played on the snare.
Note: On previous pages the snare part was beamed together with the cymbal. In order for you to see the single paradiddles more clearly the snare part is now beamed together with the bass.

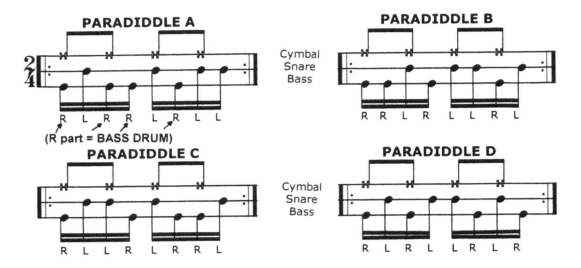

The following exercises show how you can incorporate the splitting of single paradiddles between the snare and bass while you're keeping basic rock time.

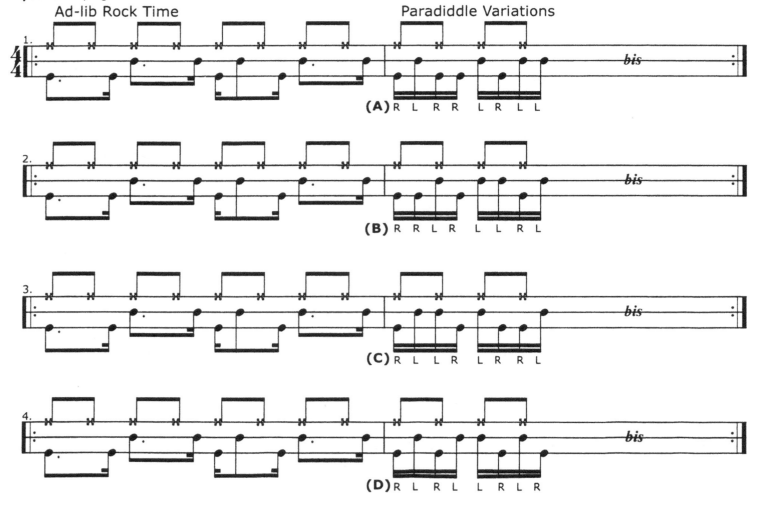

22

COMBINING THE FOUR FORMS OF THE
SINGLE PARADIDDLE BETWEEN THE SNARE AND
BASS IN COORDINATION WITH BASIC ROCK TIME

COORDINATING THREE AGAINST TWO
FOR ROCK DRUMMING

The following examples demonstrate how to play eighth triplets (*three* notes to a beat) between the bass drum and snare, while simultaneously playing the rock cymbal rhythm as regular eighth notes (*two* notes to a beat).

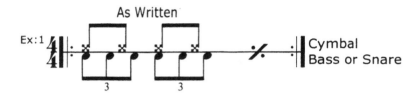

The exact positioning of the eighth-note triplet rhythm in relation to the cymbal beat in the example above can be made clearer if you relate it to parts of a sixteenth triplet.

1/8 TRIPLETS WRITTEN AS 1/16 TRIPLETS

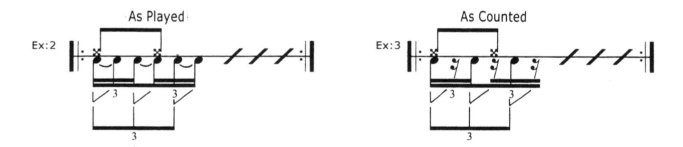

Note that each eighth triplet is worth the value of two sixteenth triplets, so it should now be perfectly clear, from examples two and three, where precisely the eighth triplet falls in relation to the regular straight eighth notes in the cymbal part.

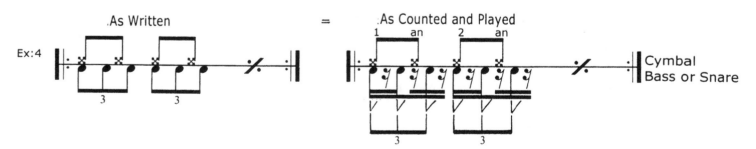

The following exercises will develop the skill to apply this concept of three against two for practical use within the framework of *slow to moderate tempo* rock music.

PRACTICAL APPLICATION OF THREE AGAINST TWO

Play one measure of an ad-lib rock beat before each exercise.

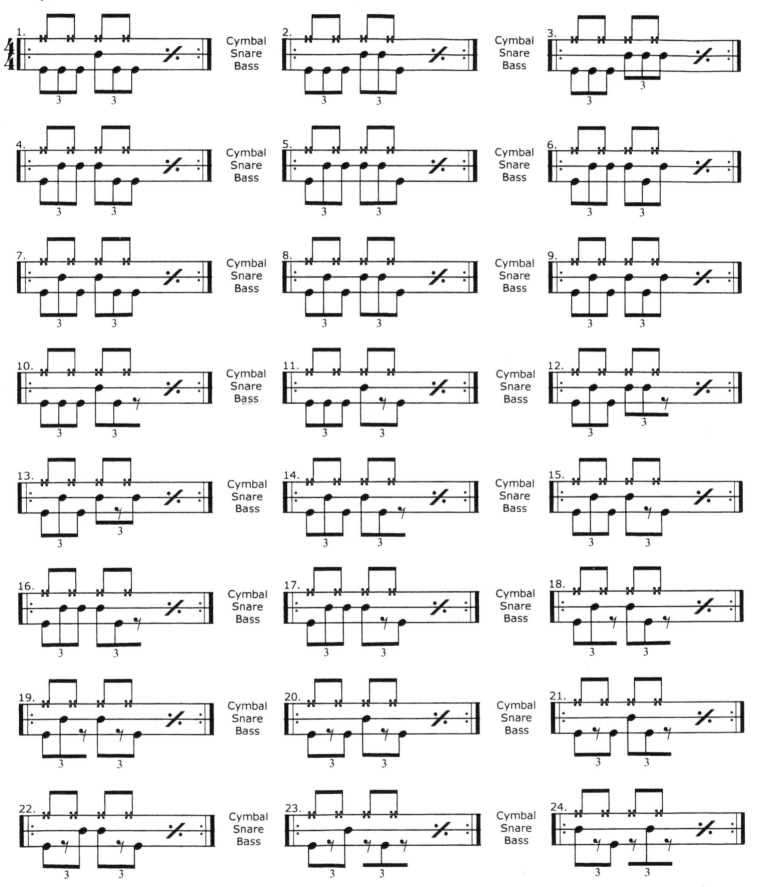

THE "INSIDE" THREE AGAINST TWO

You have seen how downbeat eighth-note triplets can be coordinated against a straight eight-note rock cymbal rhythm (three against two), and how the eighth triplet can be thought of as the 1st, 3rd, and 5th of six sixteenth-note triplets.

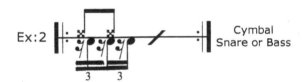

By simply playing the 2nd, 4th, and 6th of six sixteenth-note triplets you wind up with what I choose to refer to as the "inside" three.

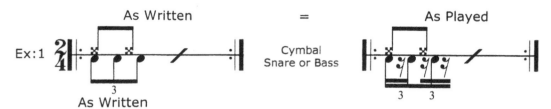

SPLITTING THE "INSIDE" THREE BETWEEN
THE SNARE AND BASS

Precede each exercise with 1½ bars of a slow ad-lib rock beat.

THREE AGAINST FOUR

The concept of two different rhythms being played simultaneously within a rock framework can be further extended to playing three against four. Instead of *eighth* triplets the *three* in this case is a *quarter* triplet (three notes over two beats) being played between the snare and bass, while the *"four"* is *two* groups of straight eighth notes played on the cymbal.

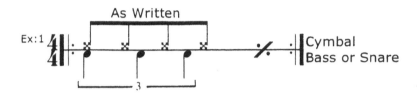

The exact positioning of the quarter triplet rhythm in relation to the cymbal beat in Example 1 is made clearer by relating it to eighth or sixteenth triplets as in the following examples.

1/4 TRIPLETS WRITTEN AS 1/8 TRIPLETS

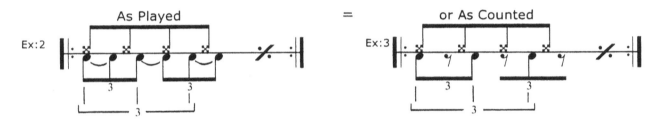

Note that each quarter triplet is worth the value of two eighth triplets.

Another way of showing the position of the 1/4 note triplet is as follows:

1/4 TRIPLETS IN RELATION TO 1/16 TRIPLETS

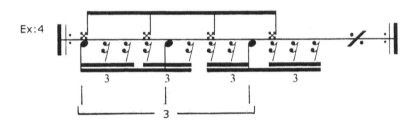

Each quarter triplet is worth the value of four sixteenth triplets.
The next group of exercises will develop facility for applying three against four *(slow to moderate tempos)* in rock music.

PRACTICAL APPLICATION OF THREE AGAINST FOUR

Play one measure of an ad-lib rock beat before each exercise.

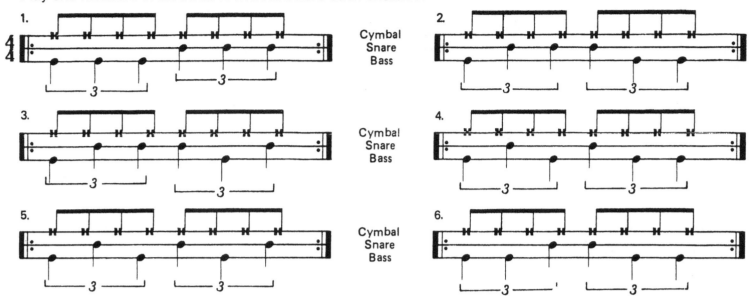

TWO AGAINST THREE COMBINED WITH
THREE AGAINST FOUR

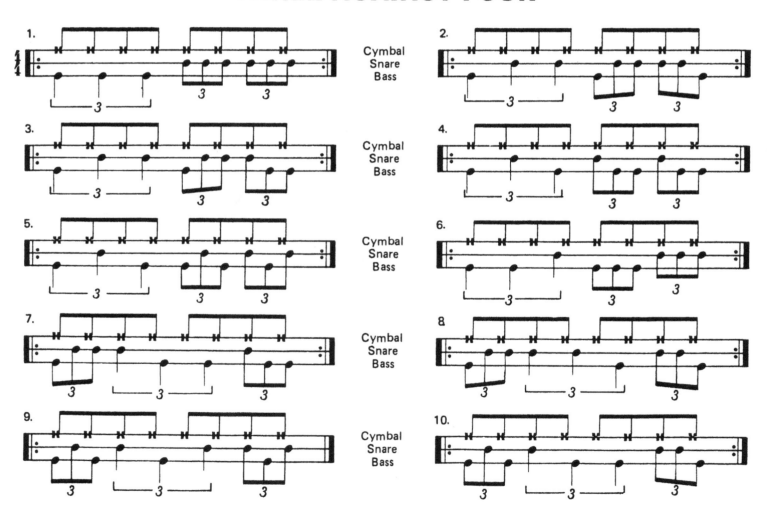

1/16 NOTE CYMBAL BEAT WITH ONE HAND
(For Slow Tempos)

Replay each exercise with the following cymbal rhythm.

VARIATIONS ON THE 1/16ᵗʰ NOTE ROCK CYMBAL RHYTHM
WITH ONE HAND

Sometimes tempos are not quite slow enough to comfortably play continual sixteenth-notes with one hand. These next two pages address the problem by demonstrating just some of the possibilities for playing a sixteenth-note cymbal beat with one hand by dropping off some of the sixteenth-notes. This will give your hand a slight break while still maintaining the overall feel of a sixteenth-note cymbal rhythm. A suggested bass drum part is included, but after playing the exercises as written play your bass in any manner you feel is appropriate and comfortable. Be sure to precede each exercise with two beats of a slow ad-lib rock beat.

For example: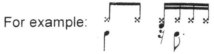

VARIATIONS CONTINUED

31

1/16 NOTE HI-HAT BEAT – ALTERNATING HANDS
(For Medium Tempos)

Note: The last five beats are not with alternating hands. They have a strong Latin flavor, and should be played on the large ride cymbal rather than the hi-hat.

SHUFFLE ROCK BEATS

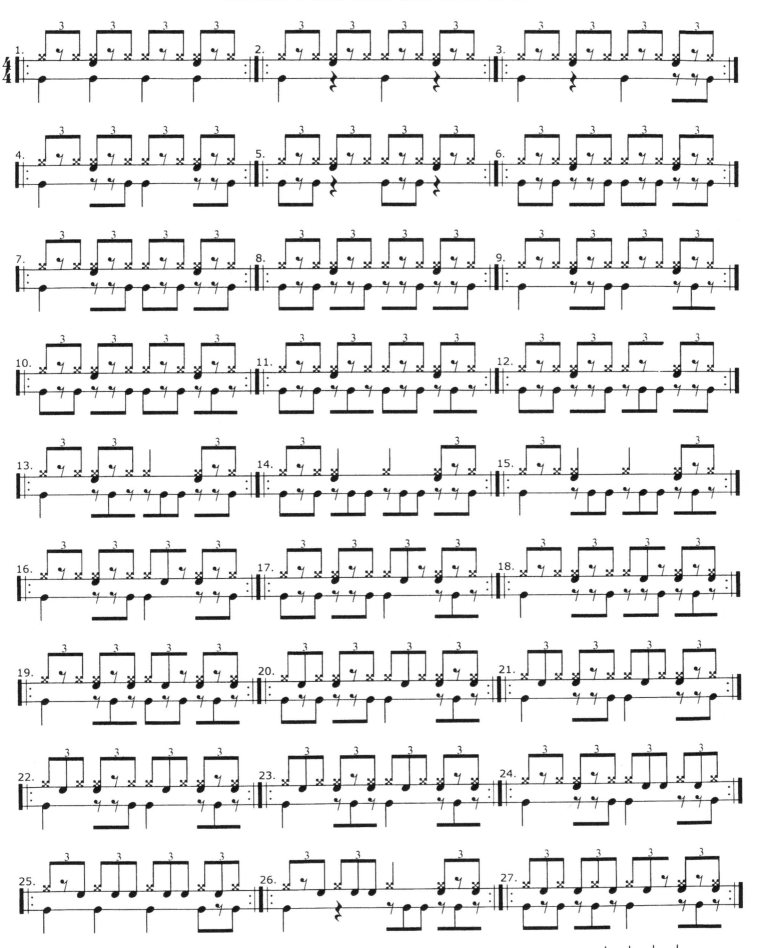

IMPORTANT: Replay exercises 1 – 15 with a straight quarter-note cymbal beat (𝄽 𝄽 𝄽 𝄽).

33

ROCK BEATS IN 3/4 TIME (WITH JUST 1/8 NOTES)

34

ROCK BEATS IN 3/4 TIME
WITH 1/16 NOTES IN THE SNARE AND BASS

A TASTE OF ROCK IN 5/4 TIME

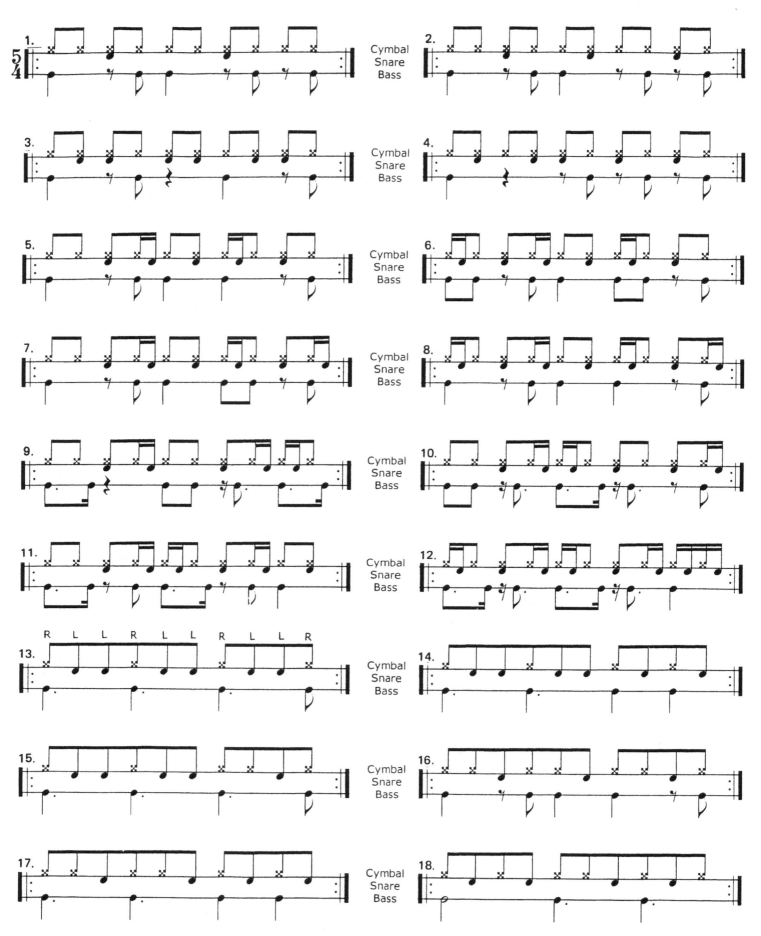

Note: Exercises 13-18 are for faster tempos ——— the snare part is played with the left hand.

A TASTE OF ROCK IN 7/4 TIME

Note: Exercises 11-16 are for faster tempos.

ROCK WITH A 6/8 or 12/8 FEEL
BASIC CYMBAL PATTERNS

38

1/16 NOTE PATTERNS FOR SNARE DRUM

1/16 NOTE PATTERNS FOR BASS DRUM

1/16 NOTE PATTERNS BETWEEN THE SNARE AND BASS

ROCK COORDINATION PHRASED IN "EIGHTH" TIME
WHILE THE BASIC BEAT REMAINS IN 4/4 TIME

The following pages show how to bring some variation to the basic rock beat by constructing one-bar phrases of coordinated rhythm uncommon to 4/4 time. One bar of 4/4 time contains the equivalent of *four* quarter-notes or *eight* eighth notes, with the quarter-note representing one beat. Since the phrasing of the coordination will be in *eighth time,* however, the time signature will be changed from 4/4 to 8/8 time for one bar. This will establish the eighth-note rather than the quarter note as the basic beat, and should make the coordinated phrases in eighth time easier to see, read. and understand.

(Notice the two bars look exactly alike and are played the same ——— only the count is changed.)

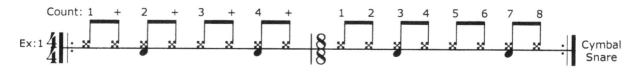

In the next two examples I have simply regrouped the eighth-notes in the second bar and changed the count according to the grouping.

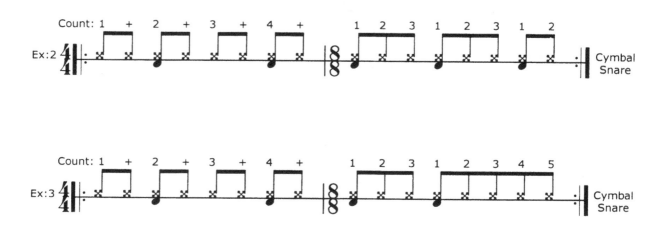

In Example 2 you can see there are two possible groups of 3/8 and one group of 2/8 that fit within one bar of 8/8 (4/4) time. Or, in Example 3 you can see there is one group of 3/8 and one group of 5/8 that fit within one bar of 8/8 (4/4) time.

Important: Be certain you understand that the groups of three eighth-notes are NOT played as triplets. They are played as straight eighth-notes, exactly the way they are played in 4/4 time ——— only the count changes, giving the feel of a 3/8 phrase.

The following pages show three bars of a coordinated rock beat in 4/4 time, followed by a one-bar variation in 8/8 time where the coordination is phrased 2/8, 3/8, or 5/8.

The same phrasing concept is employed in the next section with rock breaks.

ROCK COORDINATION PHRASED 3/8, 3/8, 2/8

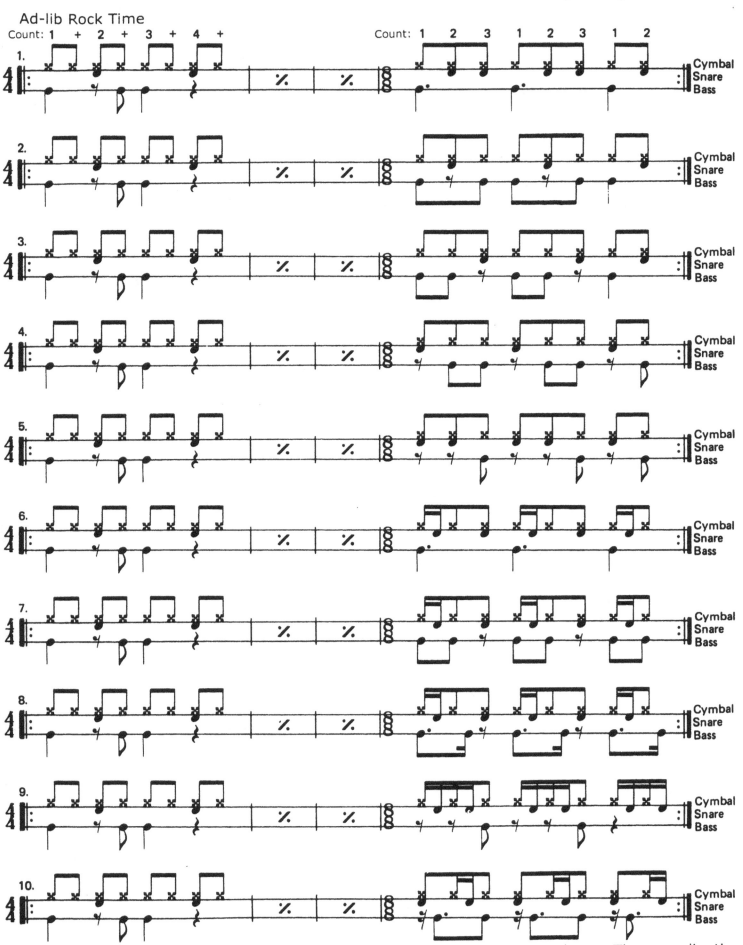

Notice that the cymbal beat remains as steady eighth-notes throughout. The coordination between the snare and bass is what brings out the variation in phrasing.

ROCK COORDINATION PHRASED 3/8, 2/8, 3/8

ROCK COORDINATION PHRASED 2/8, 3/8, 3/8

44

ROCK COORDINATION PHRASED 3/8, 5/8

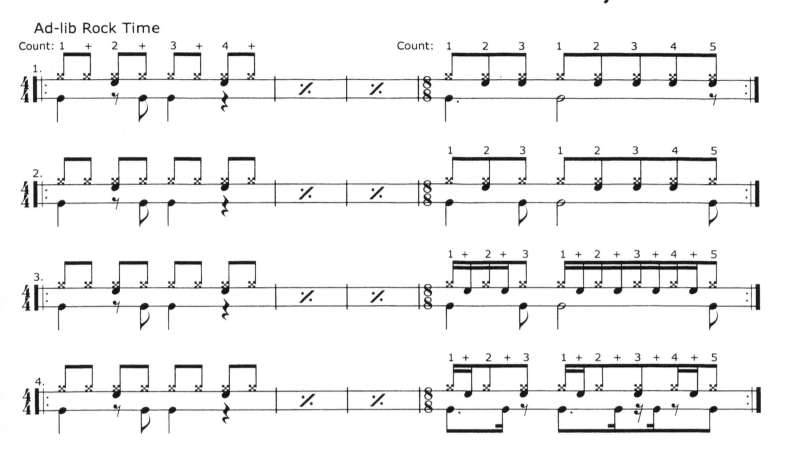

ROCK COORDINATION PHRASED 5/8, 3/8

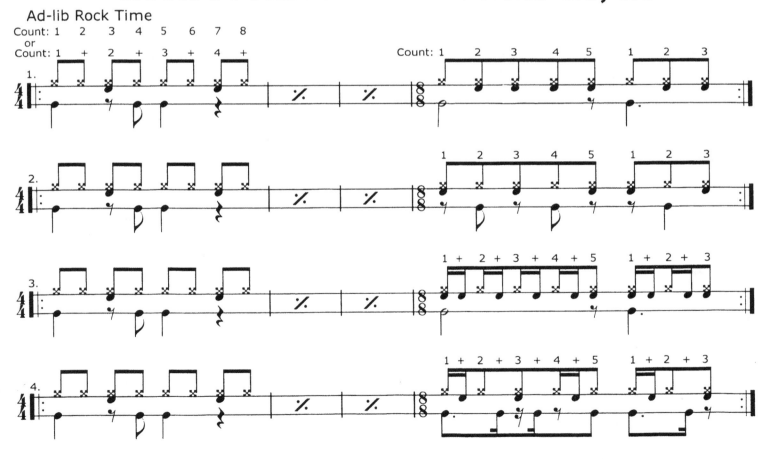

45

COORDINATION BETWEEN HI-HAT AND BASS

Until now the left foot has not been developed as a fully independent limb. On this page you will learn to coordinate the hi-hat with the ride cymbal and bass, leading into the development of hi-hat *"splashes."* Please note that since the hi-hat foot would also be used to play a second bass drum, these exercises are appropriate for developing double bass drum coordination.

Precede each exercise with 1½ bars of an ad-lib rock beat in 4/4 time.

Note: Top Line = Ride Cymbal;   Middle Line = Hi Hat;   Bottom Line = Bass Drum

FOUR-WAY COORDINATION BETWEEN THE RIDE CYMBAL, SNARE, HI-HAT AND BASS DRUM

IMPORTANT: In each exercise there is one note in parenthesis. First play the exercise with *all* the notes, then replay it leaving out the note in parenthesis.

Note: Top Line = Ride Cymbal, 2nd Line = Snare, 3rd Line = Hi-hat, Bottom Line = Bass Drum.

The above exercises are appropriate for double bass by substituting a second bass drum in place of the hi-hat part. For an in-depth study of this topic I suggest my book, **FOUR WAY INDEPENDENCE FOR ROCK DRUMMING.**

HI-HAT SPLASHES

Hi-hat splashes are commonly used when playing a basic disco feel with a steady eighth-note cymbal rhythm.

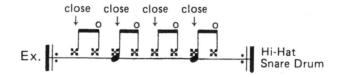

In the example above the drummer opens the hi-hat on the upbeats and closes it on the downbeats creating a splash effect for the duration of the eighth-note. (Note: The o above a note indicates when to open the hi-hat cymbals in order to achieve the splash effect. Keep the hi-hat cymbals closed on all notes without an o sign.) Play your bass drum on all downbeats.

I suggest you first play the hi-hat part alone in order to develop the ability to get a good *splash* sound. Once that has been achieved, incorporate the snare on two and four as notated.

As you play try singing the sound "ti" when you strike a closed hi-hat, and "tss" when you "splash" the cymbals. Doing this is especially good if you're not practicing at an actual set —— it gives you a sense of the sound and brings a more musical feel to your practicing. I've indicated these sounds in just the first three exercises.

SPLASHES ON UPBEAT EIGHTH NOTES

Important: Replay exercise 15 without downbeats Ex:

SPLASHES ON DOWNBEATS 1/8 NOTES

SPLASHES ON COMBINATIONS OF
UPBEAT AND DOWNBEAT 1/8 NOTES

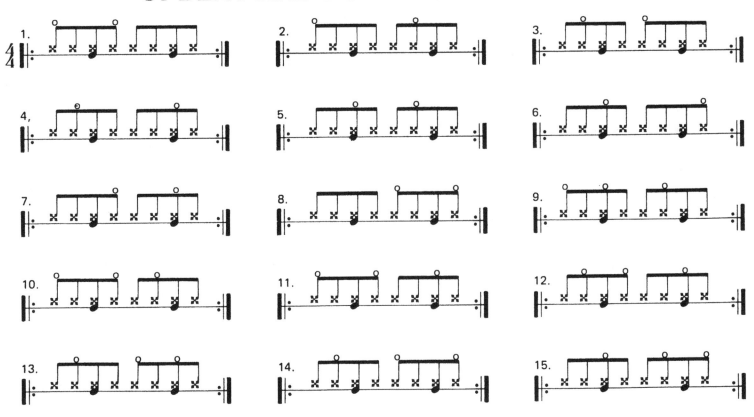

DOWNBEAT 1/4 NOTE SPLASHES COMBINED WITH UPBEAT AND DOWNBEAT 1/8 NOTE SPLASHES

*Be sure to splash the hi-hat cymbals for the full duration of a quarter-note. Keep the hi-hat closed on all notes without the o sign.

UPBEAT 1/4 NOTE SPLASHES COMBINED WITH DOWNBEAT AND UPBEAT 1/8 NOTE SPLASHES

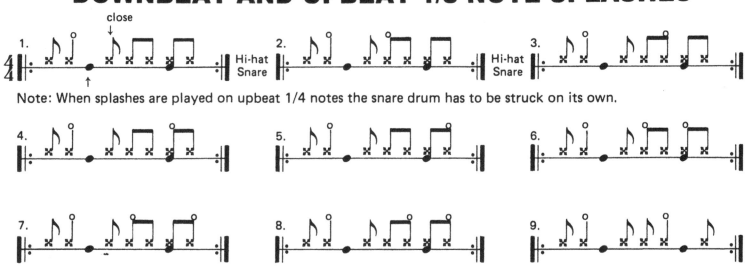

Note: When splashes are played on upbeat 1/4 notes the snare drum has to be struck on its own.

BASS DRUM VARIATIONS WITH THE HI-HAT OPENED
ON THE UPBEAT OF TWO (IN 2/4 TIME)

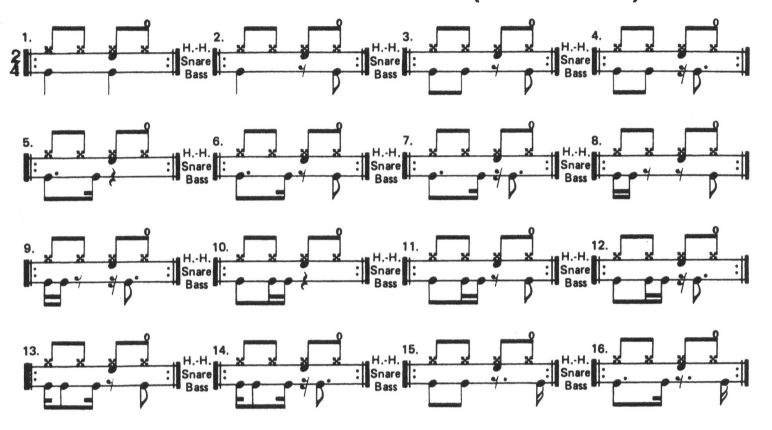

BASS DRUM VARIATIONS WITH THE HI-HAT OPENED
ON THE UPBEAT OF ONE

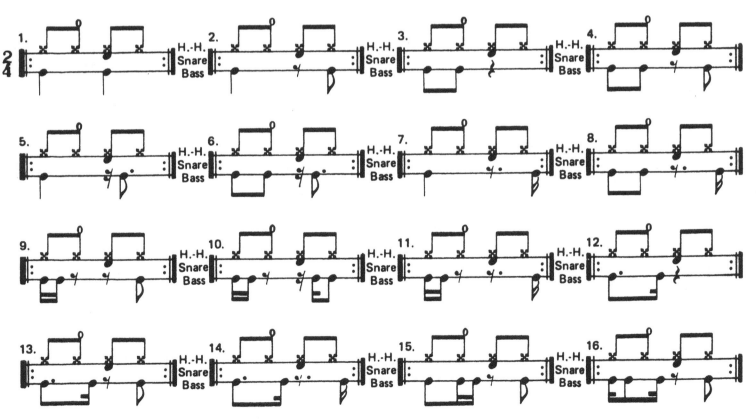

BASS DRUM VARIATIONS WITH THE HI-HAT OPENED
ON THE UPBEATS OF ONE AND TWO

BASS DRUM VARIATIONS
WITH THE HI-HAT PLAYED ONLY ON THE UPBEATS

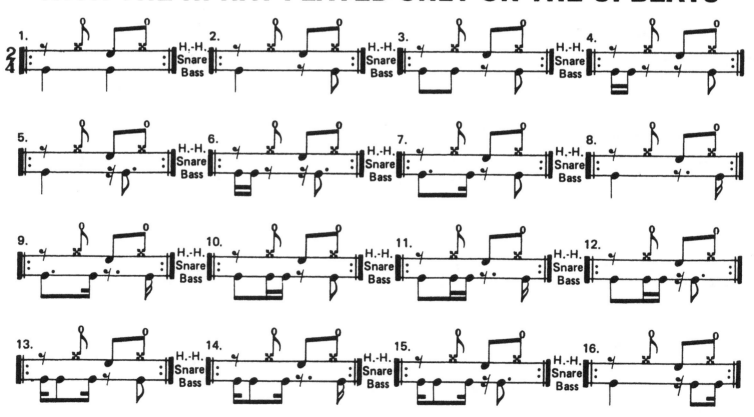

UPBEAT 1/8 NOTE SPLASHES
INTEGRATED WITH SNARE DRUM VARIATIONS

Try to accent the snare on two and four, and play all other snare notes with less force, as "ghost" notes.

53

SPLASHES ON THE UPBEAT OF ONE
INTEGRATED WITH VARIATIONS FOR SNARE AND BASS

SPLASHES ON THE UPBEAT OF TWO
INTEGRATED WITH VARIATIONS FOR SNARE AND BASS

SPLASHES WITH A 1/16 NOTE HI-HAT RHYTHM
Played With One Hand For Slow Tempos

SPLASHES WITH 1/16 NOTE HI-HAT RHYTHM
With Alternating Hands For Medium Tempos

ROCK BREAKS
ROCK BREAKS WITH 1/16 NOTES

Play one measure of an ad lib rock beat before each exercise.

For the next two pages play your bass drum in any manner you feel is appropriate and comfortable.

1/16 NOTE ROCK BREAKS WITH TIES

Play one measure of an ad lib rock beat before each exercise.

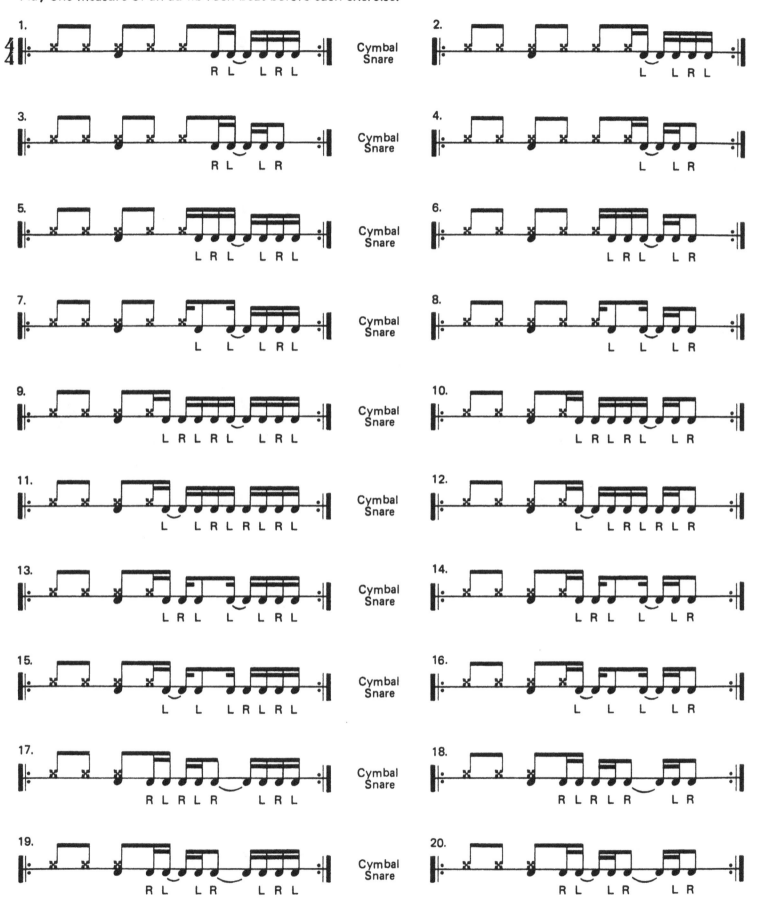

1/16 NOTE ROCK BREAKS FEATURING THE LEFT HAND

Play one-bar of ad-lib rock rhythm before each exercise.

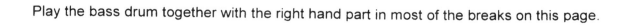

Play the bass drum together with the right hand part in most of the breaks on this page.

ROCK BREAKS WITH FLAMS

Play one measure of an ad lib rock beat before each exercise.

ROCK BREAKS WITH 1/16 NOTE TRIPLETS

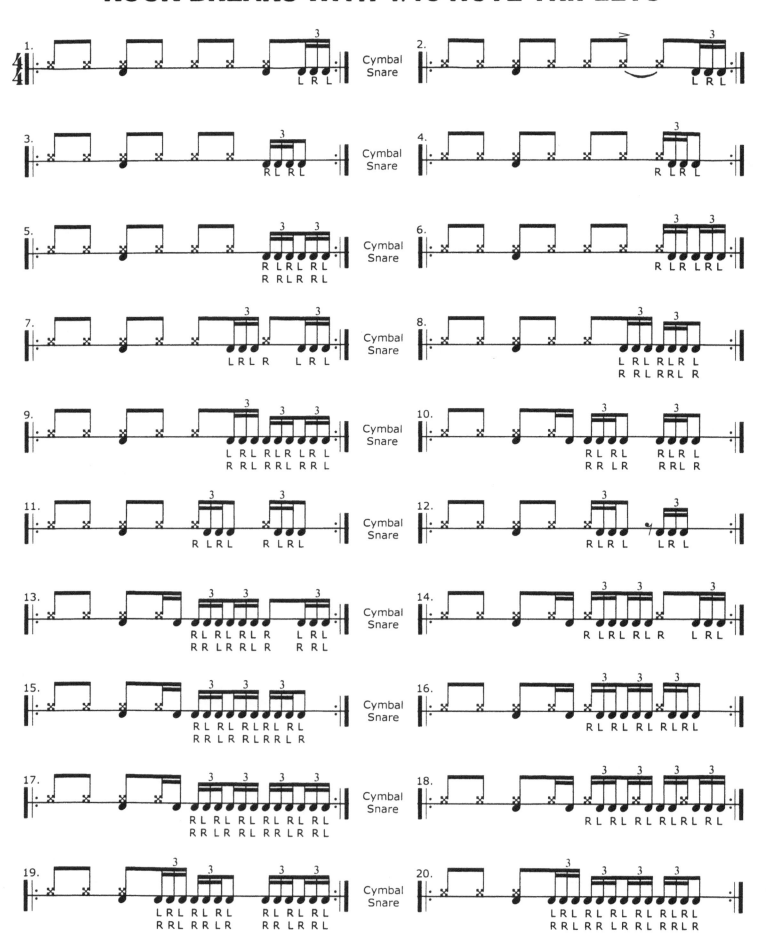

ROCK BREAKS WITH 1/16 NOTES
AND 1/16 TRIPLETS

Precede each bar with one bar of ad lib rock time.

SNARE-BASS ROCK BREAKS WITHIN TWO BEATS WITH 16TH NOTES
(HANDS PLAYED TOGETHER ON CYMBAL & SNARE DURING THE BREAKS)

Precede each exercise with one bar of ad-lib rock time.

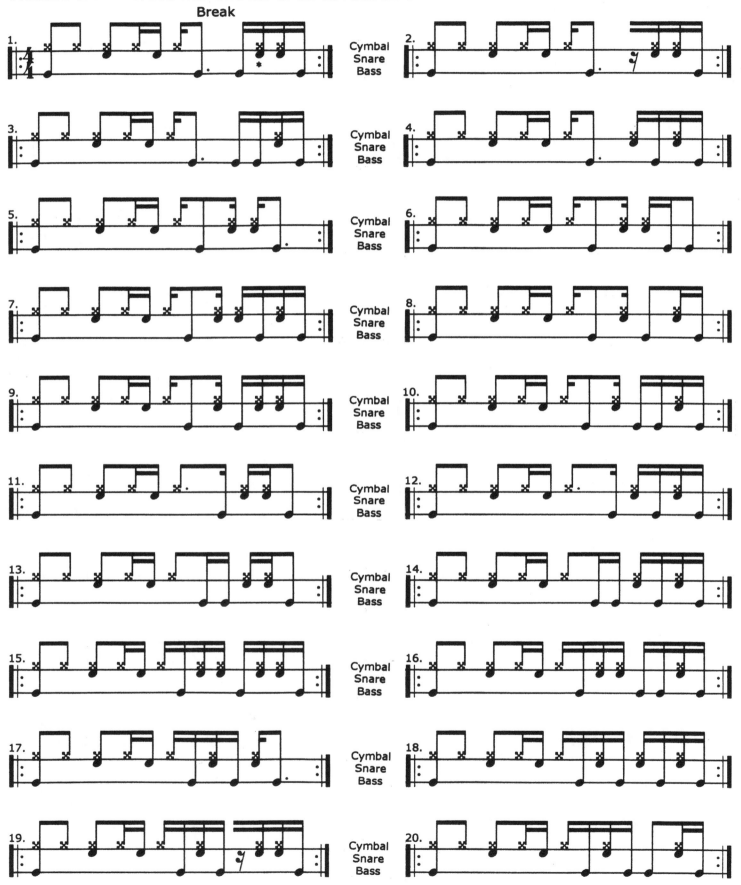

* Replay each exercise by playing flams instead of hands together during the rock break.

SNARE-BASS ROCK BREAKS WITHIN THREE BEATS WITH 16TH NOTES
(HANDS PLAYED TOGETHER ON CYMBAL & SNARE DURING THE BREAKS)

IMPORTANT: First play each exercise as written, with *all* the notes. Then replay the exercise and *OMIT* the notes in parenthesis.

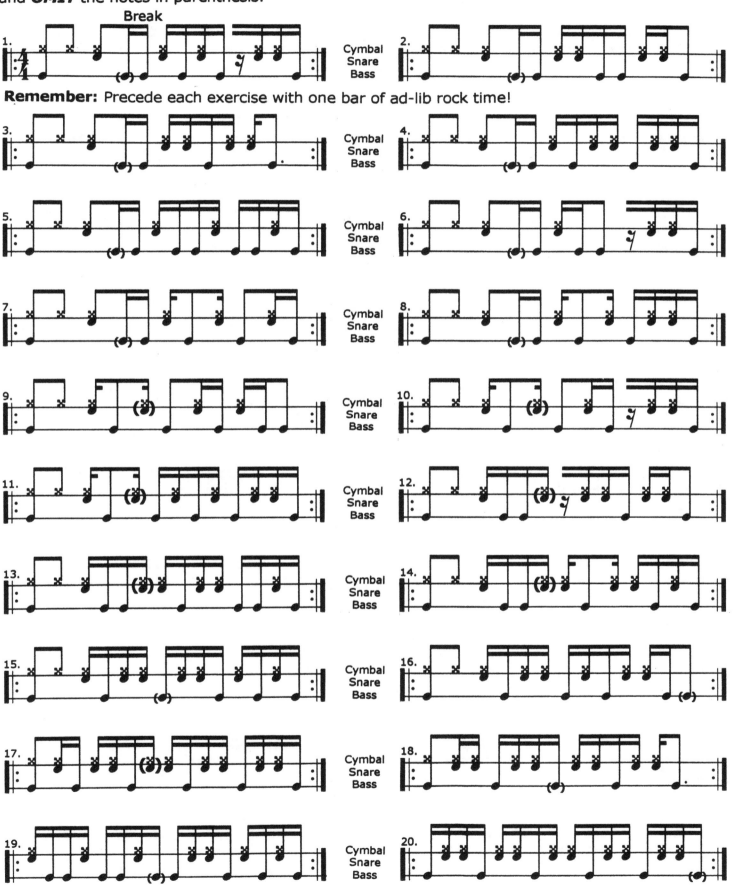

Remember: Precede each exercise with one bar of ad-lib rock time!

HAND-FOOT WARMUP IN PREPARATION FOR ROCK BREAKS WITH 16TH NOTES USING ALTERNATING HANDS

IMPORTANT: First play each exercise with *all* the notes, including those in parenthesis. Then replay each exercise and *omit* the note in parenthesis.

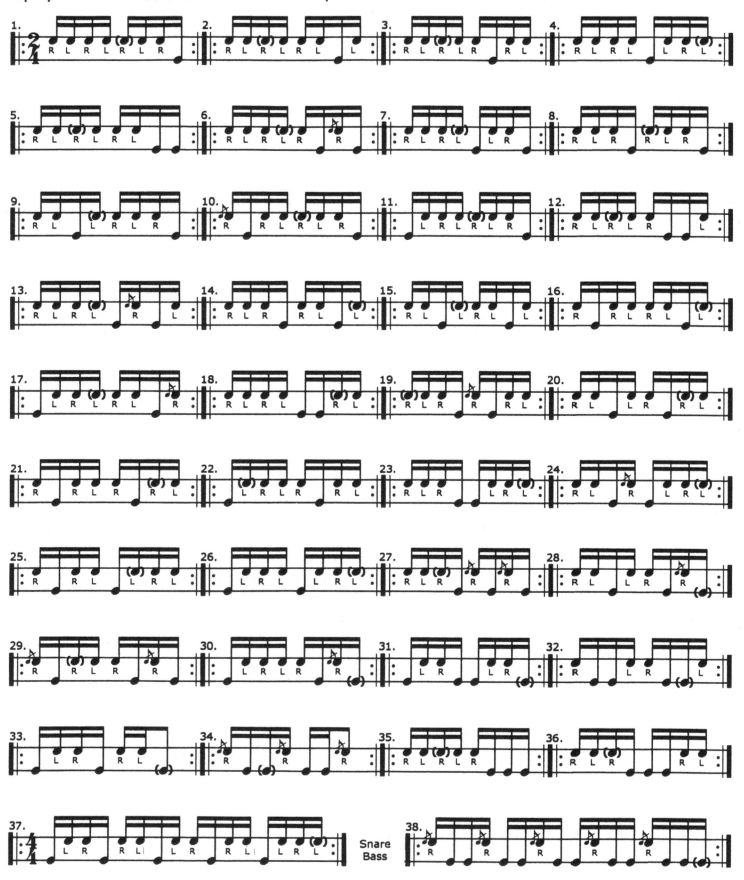

Snare
Bass

66

SNARE-BASS ROCK BREAKS WITH 16TH NOTES
(Snare Part Played With Alternating Hands)

IMPORTANT: Play each exercise as written with *all* the notes, including those in parenthesis. Then repeat the exercise and *OMIT* the notes in parenthesis.

Precede each exercise with one bar of ad-lib rock time.

Note: All sticking is optional. Use whatever sticking is most comfortable for you.

SNARE-BASS ROCK BREAKS
WITH 16TH NOTES CONTINUED

Precede each exercise with one bar of ad-lib rock time.

SNARE-BASS ROCK BREAKS
WITH 16TH NOTES CONTINUED

Precede each exercise with one bar of ad-lib rock time.

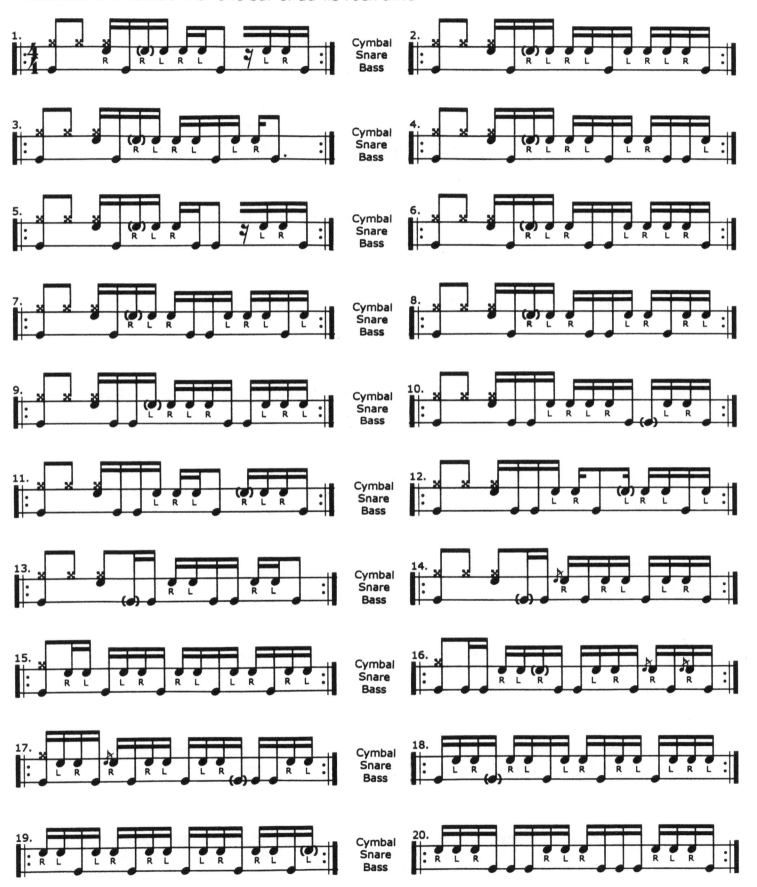

HAND-FOOT WARMUP IN PREPARATION FOR ROCK BREAKS WITH 16TH TRIPLETS USING ALTERNATING HANDS

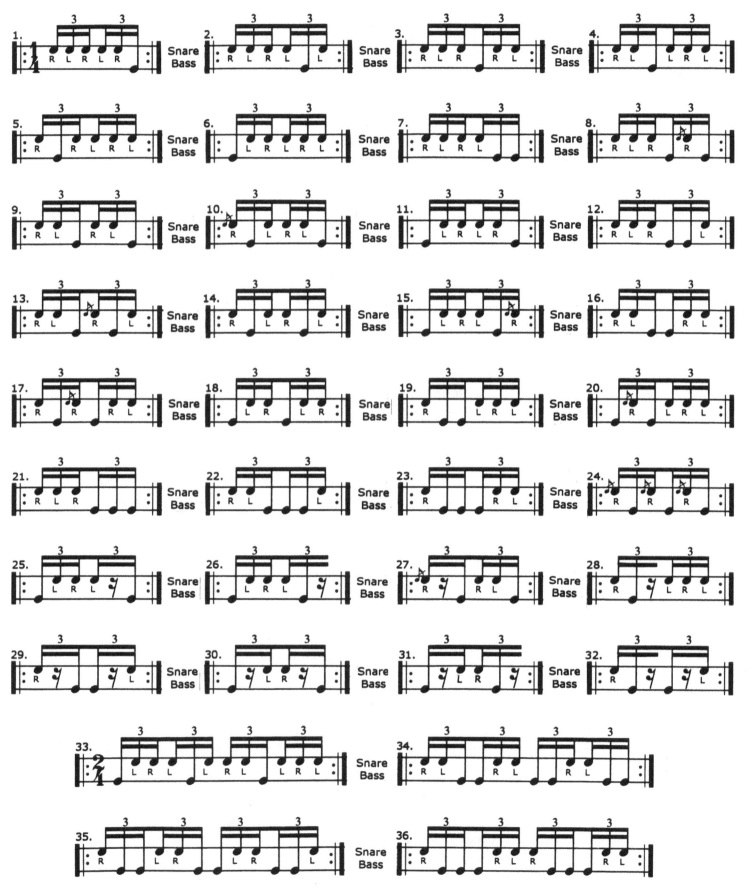

HAND-FOOT ROCK BREAKS
WITH 16TH TRIPLETS FOR SLOWER TEMPOS

Precede each exercise with one bar of ad-lib rock time.

Since the 16th note triplet breaks are for slower tempos, try preceding each break with a 16th note rock cymbal rhythm such: ♩ ♩ ♩ ♩ Break.

Note: All notated sticking is optional.

HAND-FOOT ROCK BREAKS
WITH 16TH TRIPLETS CONTINUED

Precede each exercise with one bar of ad-lib rock time.

HAND-FOOT ROCK BREAKS
WITH 16TH TRIPLETS CONTINUED

IMPORTANT: First play each exercise as written, with *all* the notes. Then replay the exercise and *omit* the notes in parenthesis.

Precede each exercise with one bar of ad-lib rock time!

ONE-BAR ROCK BREAKS WITH SINGLE PARADIDDLES

FOUR BASIC SINGLE PARADIDDLES

Play one bar of an ad-lib rock beat before each one-bar break.

PARADIDDLE A (DIDDLES AT THE END)

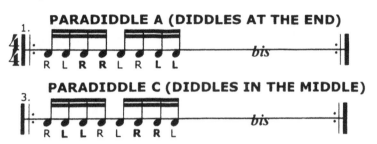

PARADIDDLE B (DIDDLES AT THE START)

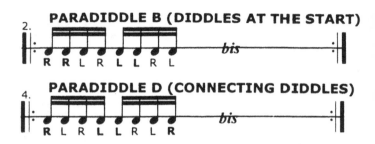

PARADIDDLE C (DIDDLES IN THE MIDDLE)

PARADIDDLE D (CONNECTING DIDDLES)

COMBINATIONS OF BASIC SINGLE PARADIDDLES

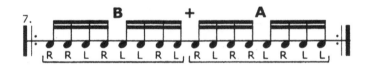

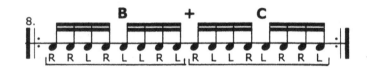

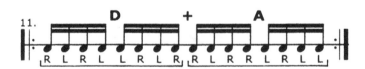

COMBINATIONS OF PARTS OF THE BASIC SINGLE PARADIDDLES

Try splitting the paradiddles between the drums by playing the right hand part on any tom tom, and the left hand part on the snare.

Important: I suggest you sing "ba" as you play the right hand part. This will bring a more musical feel to the one-bar breaks.

Ex:
```
R L R R L R L L
ba   ba ba ba
```

Play your bass in any way you feel is comfortable and appropriate.

ONE-BAR ROCK BREAKS WITH SINGLE PARADIDDLES
SPLIT BETWEEN THE SNARE AND BASS

FOUR BASIC SINGLE PARADIDDLES

Play one bar of an ad-lib rock beat before each one-bar break.

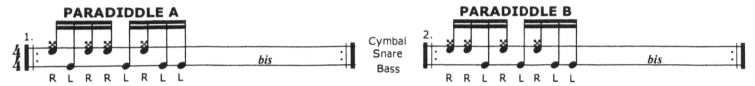

Note: The right hand part of the paradiddle is played with both hands together on the cymbal and snare, while the left hand part is played with the bass foot.

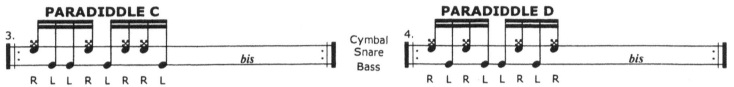

COMBINATIONS OF THE 4 BASIC PARADIDDLES

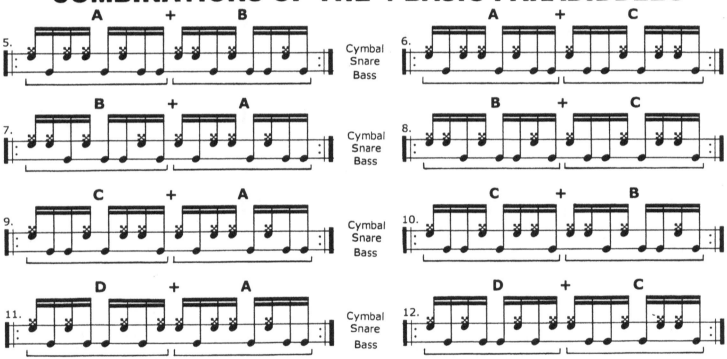

COMBINATIONS OF PARTS OF THE 4 PARADIDDLES

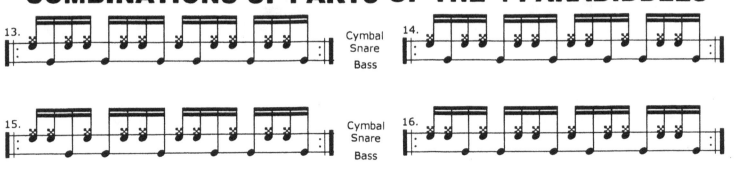

BREAKS WITH 5 STROKE ROLLS (OPEN DOUBLE STROKES)

Note: Even though one **R** or **L** is placed under a note with a slash, be sure to play that note as a double stroke and double the rhythm, as shown in the example above.

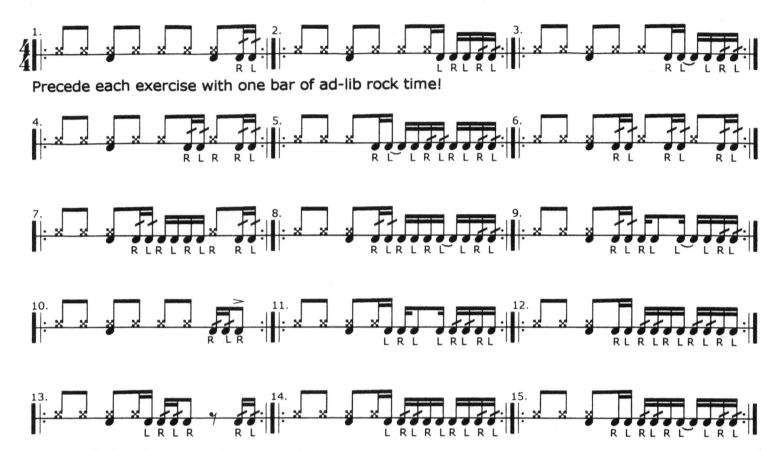

Precede each exercise with one bar of ad-lib rock time!

Note: All the above breaks either started or ended on the count of one (the downbeat) or "an" (the upbeat). The remaining breaks feature what I choose to refer to as "inside" fives — they either start or end on the counts of "E" and "D". After playing the rolls with double strokes, replay them using single strokes.

76

BREAKS WITH 7 & 5 STROKE ROLLS (OPEN DOUBLE STROKES)

Precede each exercise with one bar of ad-lib rock rhythm.

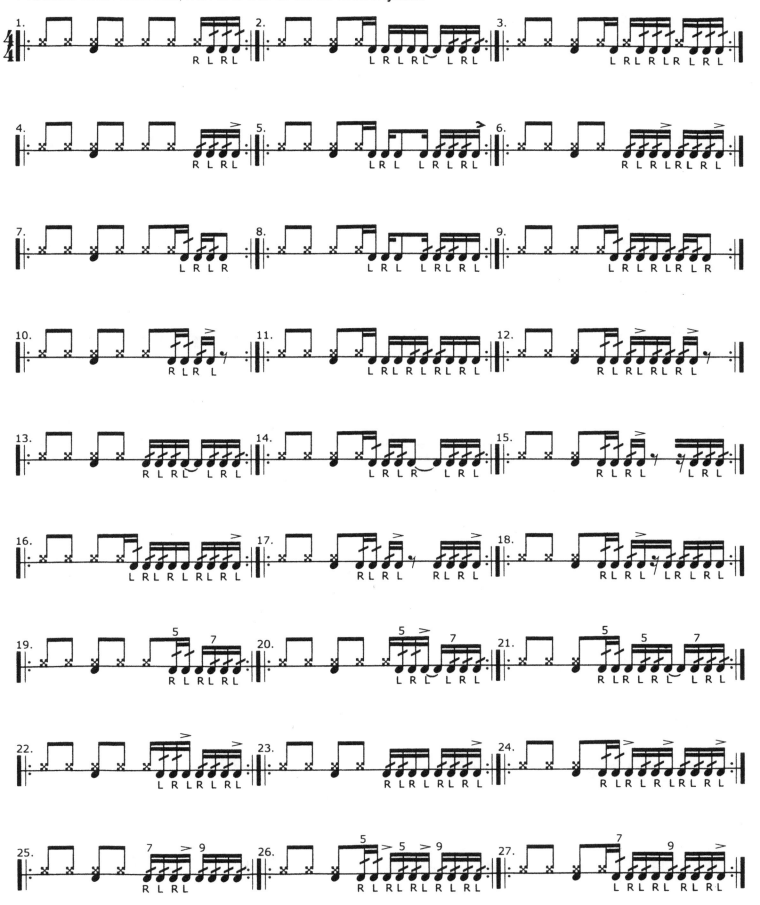

5 STROKE ROLLS (DOUBLES) WITH BASS KICKS

IMPORTANT: First play each exercise as written, with **all** the notes, including those in parenthesis. Then replay the exercise and **omit** the notes in parenthesis.

Precede each exercise with one bar of ad-lib rock time.

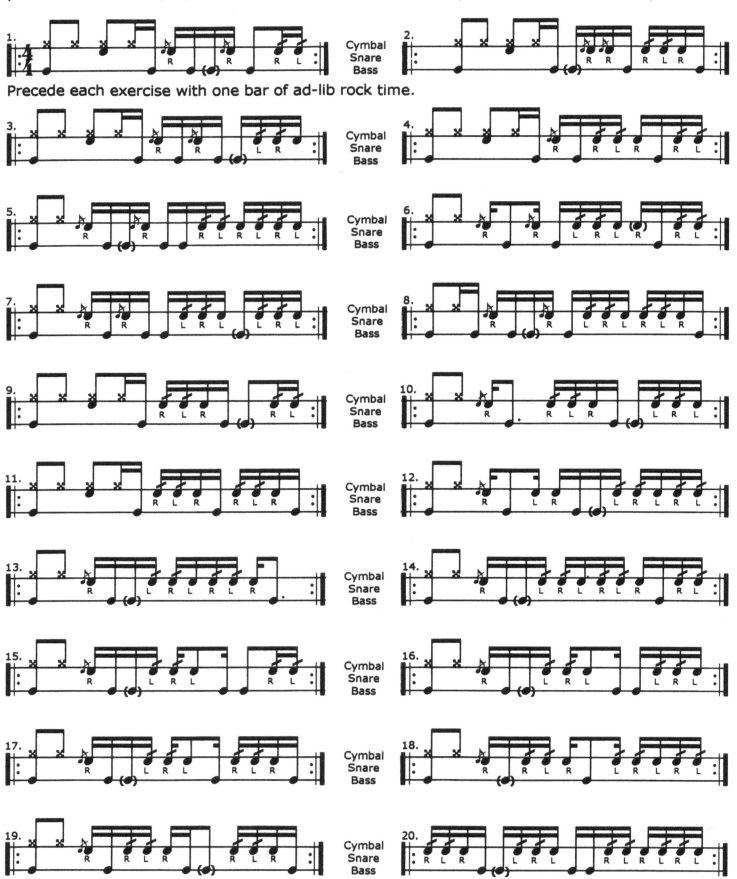

7 STROKE OPEN ROLLS (DOUBLES) WITH BASS KICKS

IMPORTANT: First play each exercise as written, with **all** the notes, including those in parenthesis. Then replay the exercise and **omit** the notes in parenthesis.

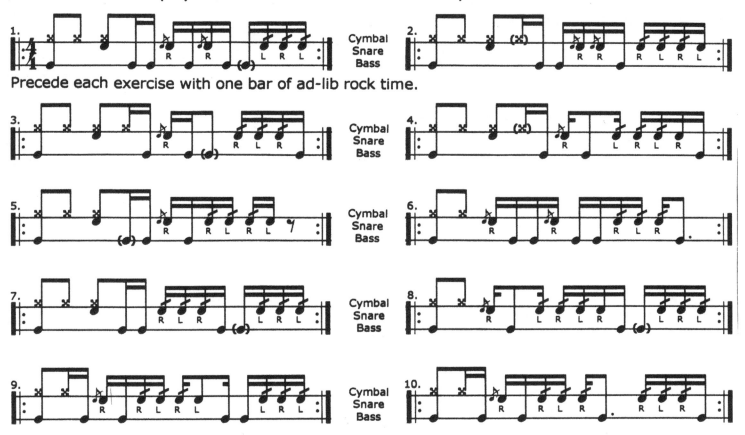

Precede each exercise with one bar of ad-lib rock time.

Note: In exercises 6, 7 and 10, the seven-stroke roll ends with a bass kick instead of on the opposite hand.

5 & 7 STROKE OPEN ROLLS (DOUBLES) WITH BASS KICKS

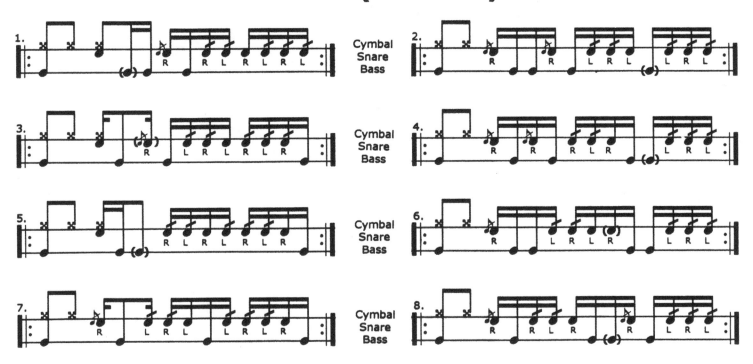

Remember: Replay each exercise and substitute single strokes in place of the double strokes.

5, 7, 9 & 11 STROKE OPEN ROLLS (DOUBLES) WITH BASS KICKS

IMPORTANT: First play each exercise as written, with **all** the notes. Then replay the exercise and **omit** the notes in parenthesis.

Precede each exercise with one bar of ad-lib rock time!

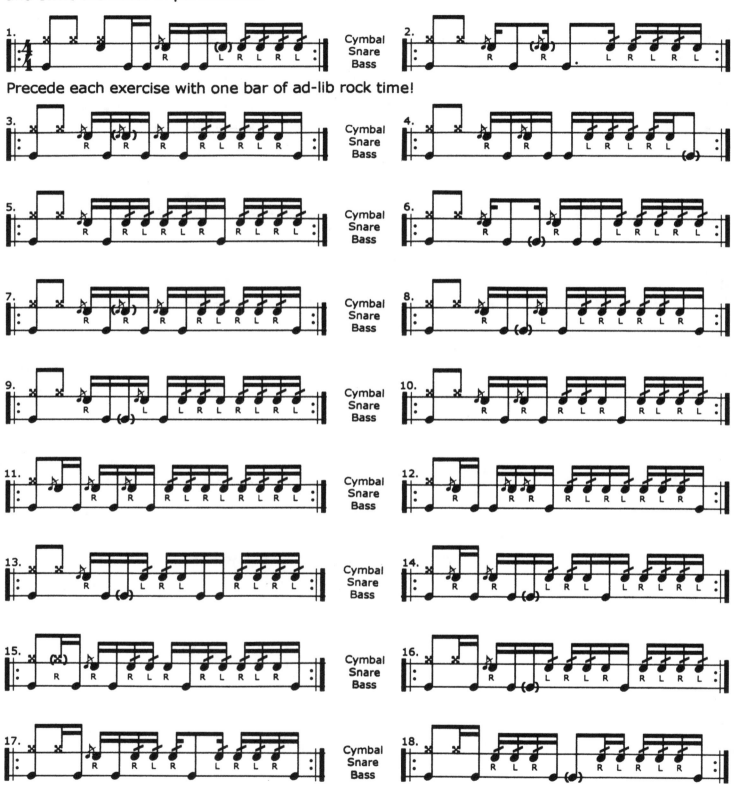

SPLITTING THE DOUBLE-STROKE IN ROCK BREAKS

When double-strokes are used in rock breaks, and divided between the snare and small tom tom, most drummers will play either four strokes or two strokes on each drum.

The double itself, however, is rarely split. You do this by playing the first of the double strokes on the **small tom tom,** while the second stroke is played on the **snare.**

(Splitting The Right Hand Double)   (Splitting The Left Hand Double)   (Splitting Both The Right Hand And Left Hand Double)

The next two exercises show the double stroke split between the large tom tom and snare. This is more difficult because the distance from the large (floor) tom tom to the snare is greater than the distance between the small (bass) tom tom and the snare.

Note: Only the right hand double-stroke can be split between the floor tom tom and snare ———it's not possible to do with the left hand.

At first glance Exercises 3 - 7 look deceptively easy, but try playing them from behind a drum set, at a speed that can be used in a rock break, and you soon discover just how difficult it is. First practice the exercises as written, then try playing them as one-bar rock breaks by playing one bar of an ad-lib rock beat before each exercise. Obviously, they can be used in longer solos, as well as in the jazz idiom. Once you're able to split the double strokes between the snare and tom toms during actual performance you join an elite club of relatively few drummers who have achieved this skill.

ROCK BREAKS WITH A 6/8 or 12/8 FEEL

HAND-FOOT ROCK BREAKS WITH A 6/8 OR 12/8 FEEL

IMPORTANT: First play each exercise with **all** the notes, including those in parenthesis. Then replay each exercise and **omit** the note in parenthesis.

HAND-FOOT ROCK BREAKS WITH A 6/8 OR 12/8 FEEL CONTINUED

IMPORTANT: First play each exercise with *all* the notes, including those in parenthesis. Then replay each exercise and *omit* the note in parenthesis.

HAND-FOOT ROCK BREAKS WITH A 6/8 OR 12/8 FEEL CONTINUED

IMPORTANT: First play each exercise with **all** the notes, including those in parenthesis. Then replay each exercise and **omit** the note in parenthesis.

ROCK BREAKS WITH 3 STROKE RUFFS (32ND NOTES)

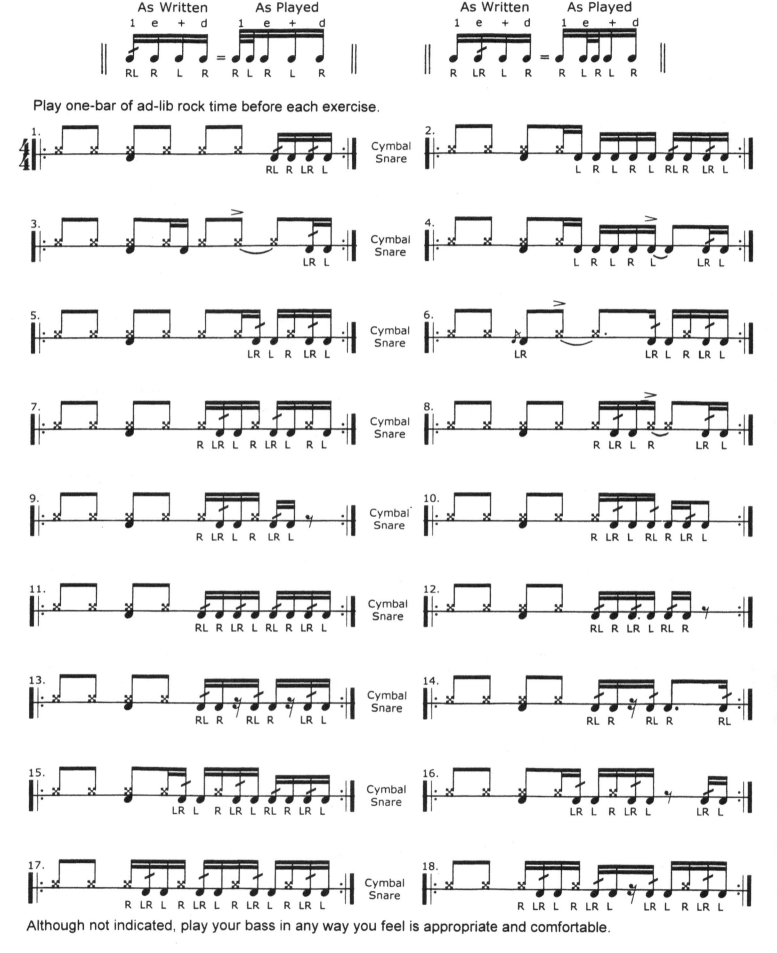

Play one-bar of ad-lib rock time before each exercise.

Although not indicated, play your bass in any way you feel is appropriate and comfortable.

ROCK BREAKS WITH THREE-STROKE RUFFS AND BASS KICKS

Precede each exercise with one bar of ad-lib rock time.

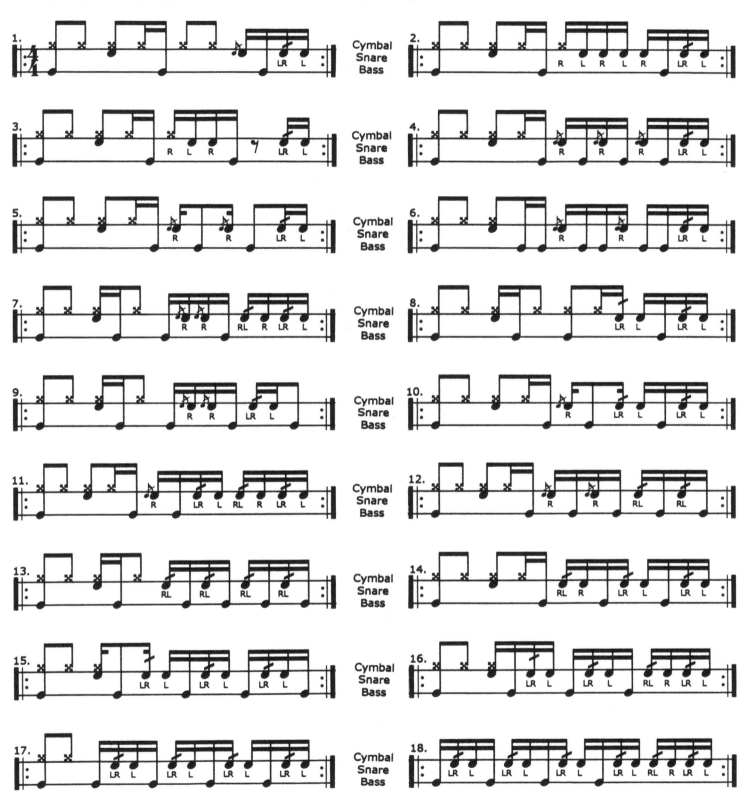

ROCK BREAKS WITH 4 STROKE RUFFS

Play one-bar of *slow* ad-lib rock time before each exercise.

Play your bass in any way you feel is appropriate and comfortable.

ROCK BREAKS WITH FOUR-STROKE RUFFS AND BASS KICKS

Precede each exercise with one bar of ad-lib rock time.

All sticking is optional.

ONE-MEASURE ROCK BREAKS PHRASED 3/8, 3/8, 2/8

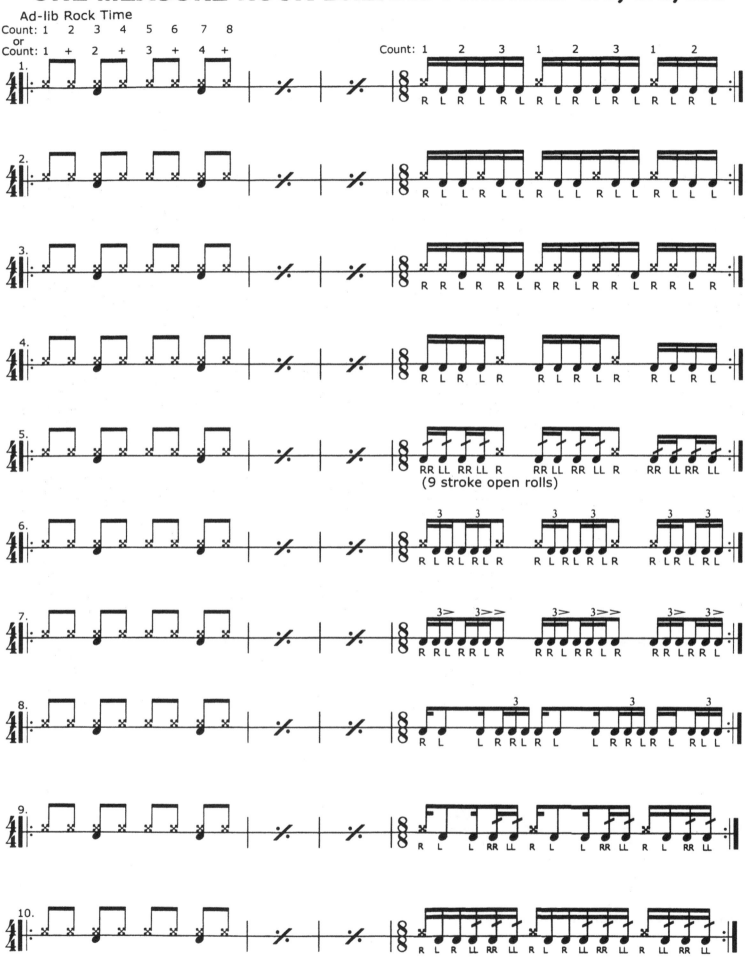

ONE-MEASURE ROCK BREAKS WITH BASS KICKS
PHRASED 3/8, 3/8, 2/8

ONE-MEASURE ROCK BREAKS PHRASED 3/8, 2/8, 3/8

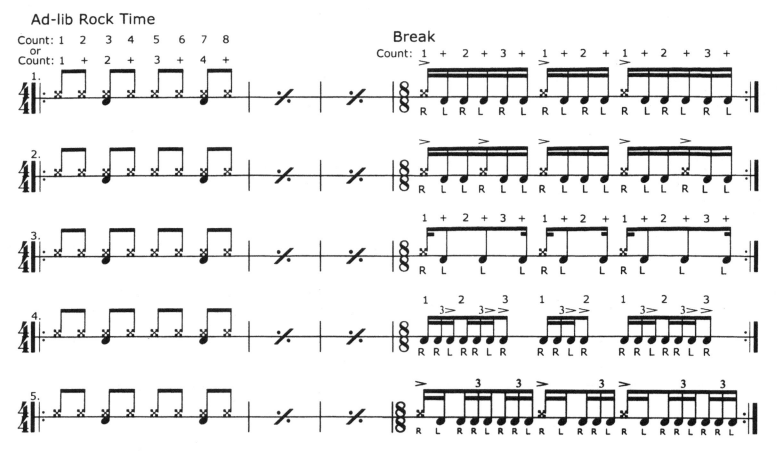

ONE-MEASURE ROCK BREAKS WITH BASS KICKS
PHRASED 3/8, 2/8, 3/8

ONE-MEASURE ROCK BREAKS PHRASED 2/8, 3/8, 3/8

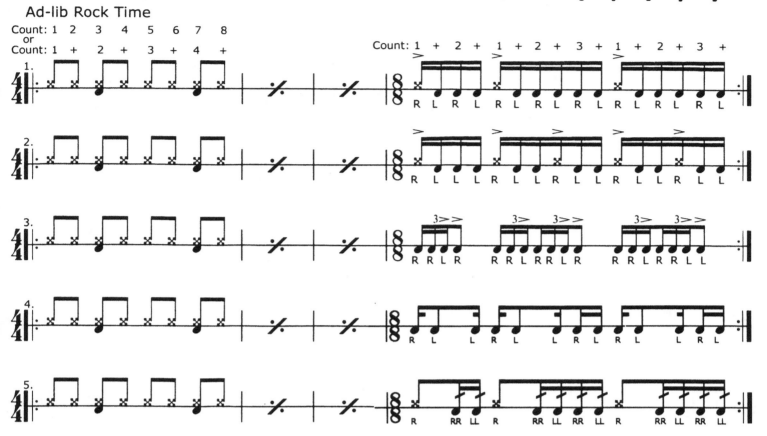

ONE-MEASURE ROCK BREAKS WITH BASS KICKS PHRASED 2/8, 3/8, 3/8

ONE-MEASURE ROCK BREAKS PHRASED 3/8, 5/8

ONE-MEASURE ROCK BREAKS WITH BASS KICKS
PHRASED 3/8, 5/8

ONE-MEASURE ROCK BREAKS PHRASED 5/8, 3/8

ONE-MEASURE ROCK BREAKS WITH BASS KICKS PHRASED 5/8, 3/8

ROCK BREAKS WITH 1/16 QUINTUPLETS
(SLOW TO MODERATE TEMPOS)

Play one-bar of ad-lib rock rhythm before each exercise.

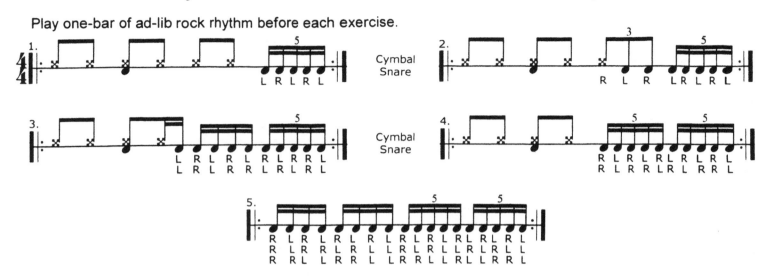

ROCK BREAKS DOUBLING 1/16 QUINTUPLETS (10's)
(SLOW TO MODERATE TEMPOS)

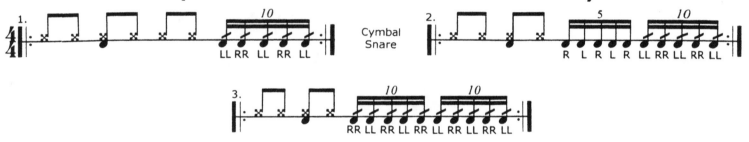

ROCK BREAKS WITH 1/8 NOTE QUINTUPLETS
OVER TWO BEATS

Rock Break doubling the 1/8 note quintuplet.

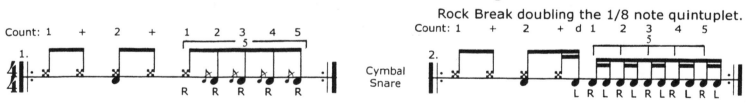

ROCK BREAKS WITH SEPTUPLETS

A 1/16 note septuplet within one beat for slow tempos.

A 1/8 note septuplet over two beats for moderate tempos.

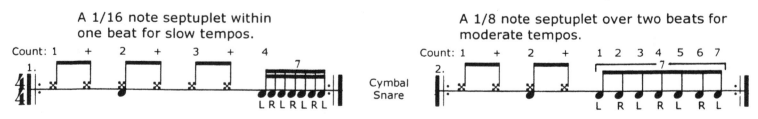

An in-depth presentation of this topic is presented in my book, **ROCK DRUMMING WITH QUINTUPLETS.**

A TASTE OF LINEAR ROCK

For several years I have had numerous requests to add some pages dealing with linear rock drumming. The following three pages offer just a taste of the subject.

Even though linear playing has been in vogue for quite some time I still find some players asking me to explain the difference between linear and non-linear drumming. To clarify the difference, the simplest explanation I can offer is that linear drumming, in its purest form, is never striking two surfaces simultaneously. In other words, if you strike a cymbal you don't strike the snare, tom tom or bass at the same time; if you strike the snare, you don't strike the bass, cymbal or tom tom at the same time.

The following two pages present eight different cymbal/snare patterns for two bars that will help to visually clarify the difference between linear and non-linear drumming. Each of the eight patterns is first highlighted without a bass drum part. The same patterns are then shown on the left side of the page with the snare part divided in linear fashion between the snare and bass. The right side of the page shows the same patterns with the bass drum included in a non-linear fashion.

Following on from the eight cymbal/snare patterns is a final page of 18 two-bar patterns only in linear form. There are hundreds of other possible patterns, and it's left up to the individual reader to explore some of those many possibilities.

For an in-depth presentation of linear playing for both rock and jazz drumming I suggest my following books – each of these books presents the topic in a different format:

DRUMMIN' IN THE RHYTHM OF ROCK
DRUM TREK (The Final Frontier of Rock)
LINEAR JAZZ DRUMMING
DRUMMING OUTSIDE THE BOX

PATTERN #1 (WITHOUT BASS)

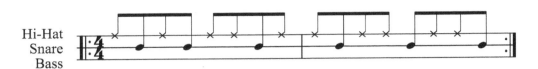

LINEAR WITH BASS   NON-LINEAR WITH BASS

PATTERN #2 (WITHOUT BASS)

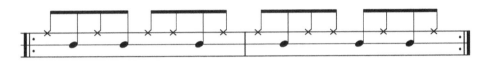

LINEAR WITH BASS   NON-LINEAR WITH BASS

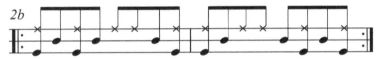

PATTERN #3 (WITHOUT BASS)

LINEAR WITH BASS   NON-LINEAR WITH BASS

PATTERN #4 (WITHOUT BASS)

LINEAR WITH BASS   NON-LINEAR WITH BASS

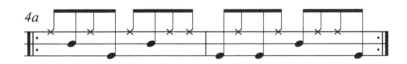

PATTERN #5 (WITHOUT BASS)

LINEAR WITH BASS

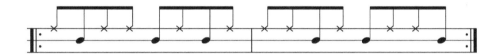

NON-LINEAR WITH BASS

PATTERN #6 (WITHOUT BASS)

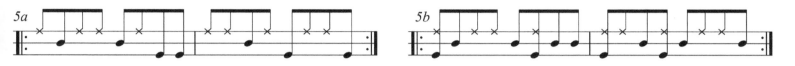

LINEAR WITH BASS

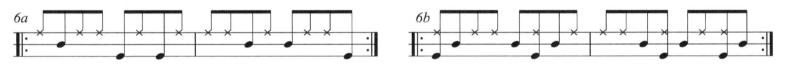

NON-LINEAR WITH BASS

PATTERN #7 (WITHOUT BASS)

LINEAR WITH BASS

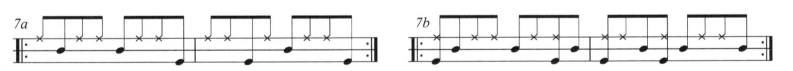

NON-LINEAR WITH BASS

PATTERN #8 (WITHOUT BASS)

LINEAR WITH BASS

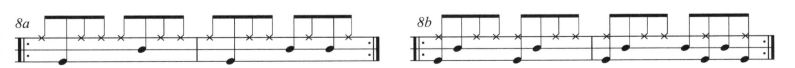

NON-LINEAR WITH BASS

TWO BAR LINEAR PATTERNS IN 4/4 TIME

Cym.
Snare
Bass

NOTE: Replay each exercise, and simply think of the 8th notes as 16th notes. The patterns would then be appropriate for playing in half time.

SUPPLEMENT

The following pages were not originally part of the book. However, I've had numerous requests to include exercises with variations for playing the hi-hat in rock, and this supplement is an answer to those requests.

The exercises are variations on the 16th note rock beat played with alternating hands on the hi-hat using open 32nd note drags and open 32nd note rolls in 2/4 time (4/4 when repeated), and 6/8 time (12/8 when repeated). The 32nd notes are written in short form with an extra slash across the stem of a 16th note allowing for fewer notated notes, making the reading somewhat easier.

Aside from learning hi-hat variations there's an added benefit - you develop the skill for playing open drags and rolls within a highly musical context.

All exercises are written just for hi-hat and snare on a single staff line. Notes above the line with an X for a note head are for hi-hat; notes below the line with a regular note head are for snare. Since the focus of the exercises is on variations for the hi-hat the snare part is simply an accented backbeat.

The sticking above the notes is for a right-handed player. If you're a lefty (southpaw) simply reverse the sticking.

No bass part is notated. After mastering each exercise as written include your bass in any way you feel is appropriate and comfortable, and use your hi-hat foot in the same way to play splashes.

One final point - the variations are not necessarily meant to be played continually - instead, they could just be included from time to time as you play the basic rock hi-hat beat. Moreover, instead of playing the variations on the hi-hat they could also be used as fills or breaks around the drums.

VARIATIONS ON THE BASIC 16th NOTE ROCK BEAT ON HI-HAT WITH OPEN 32 NOTE DRAGS

NOTE: Instead of 32nd notes being written, they'll be notated with a slash across the stem of 16th notes as follows:

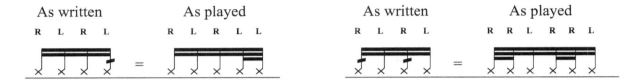

BASIC HI-HAT BEAT

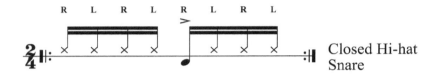

Closed Hi-hat
Snare

Precede each of the following exercises with two beats of the basic hi-hat beat.

VARIATIONS ON THE FIRST BEAT

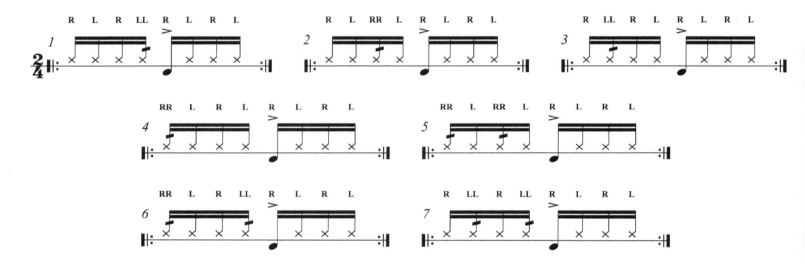

VARIATIONS ON THE SECOND BEAT

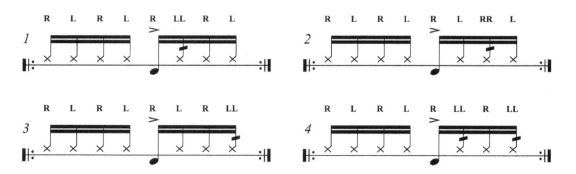

COMBINATIONS OF DRAGS
ON THE FIRST & SECOND BEAT

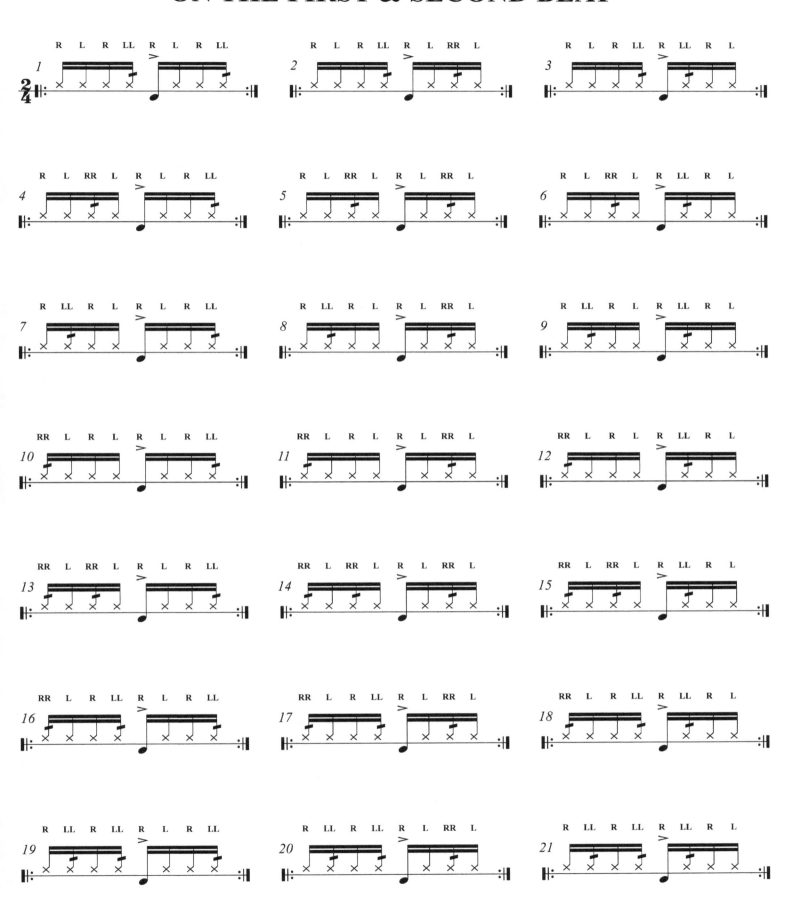

103

VARIATIONS ON THE BASIC 16th NOTE ROCK BEAT
ON HI-HAT WITH OPEN DOUBLE STROKE ROLLS

Once again, 32nd notes are notated with a slash across the stem of 16th notes. Precede each exercise with two beats of the basic 16th note rock beat on hi-hat.

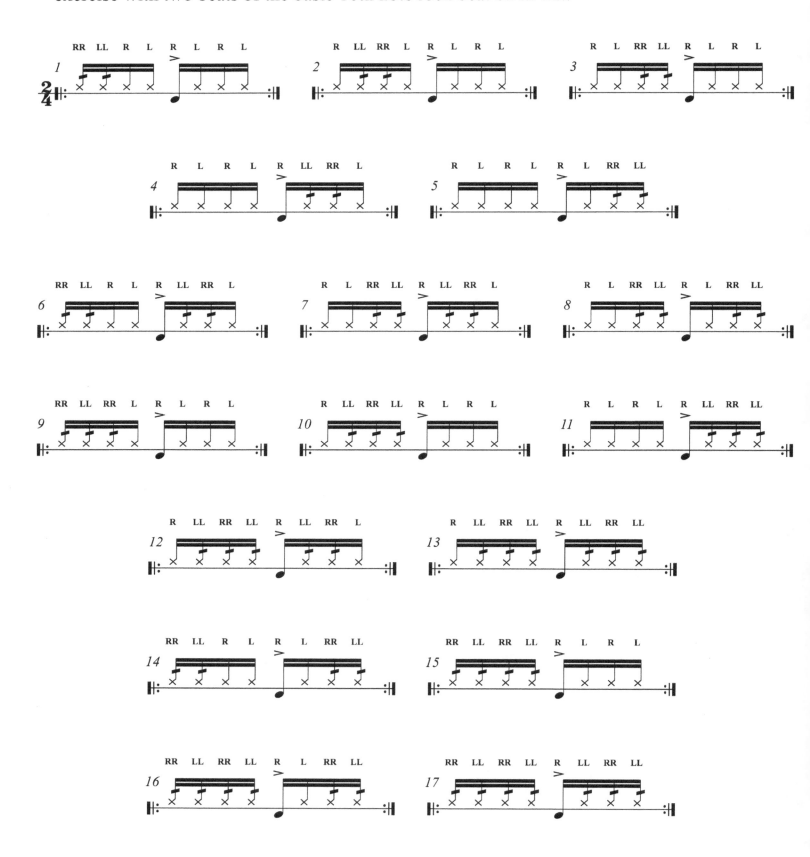

COMBINING OPEN DRAGS & OPEN ROLLS

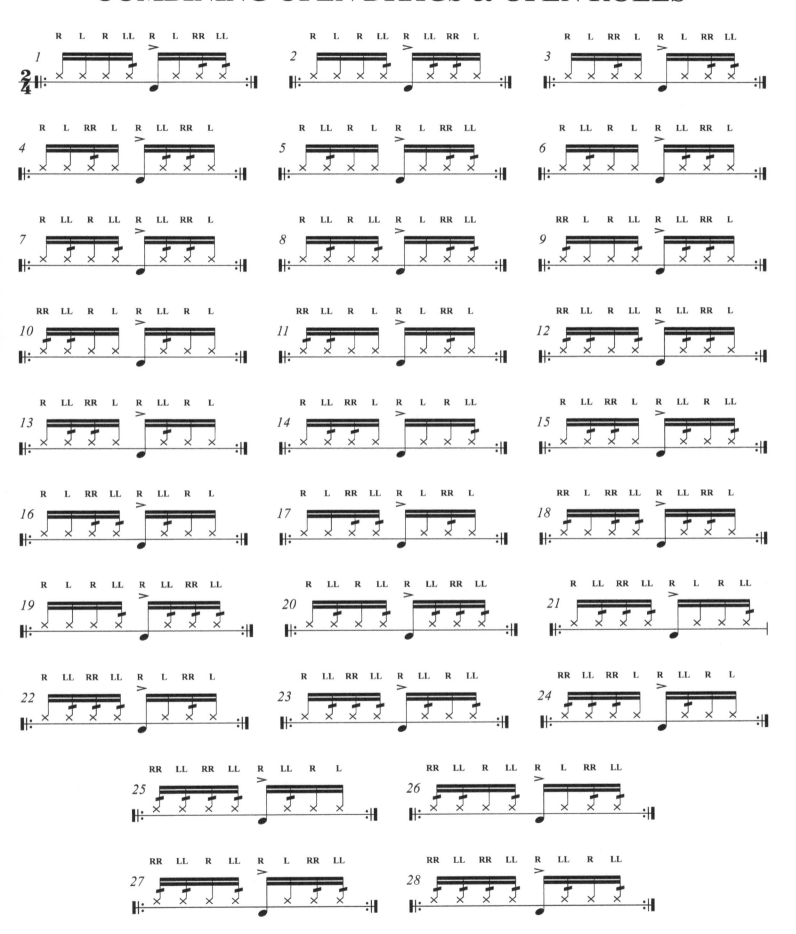

VARIATIONS ON THE BASIC 16th NOTE
ROCK HI-HAT BEAT WITH ALTERNATING HANDS
& OPEN ROLLS IN 6/8 TIME

BASIC BEAT

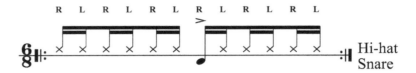

IMPORTANT: Play the notes with an extra slash across their stems as double strokes.

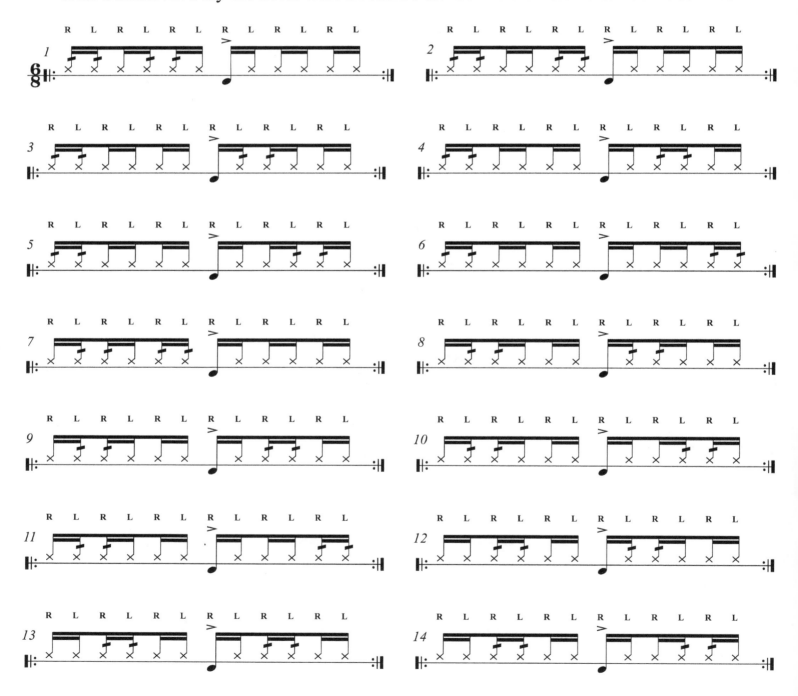

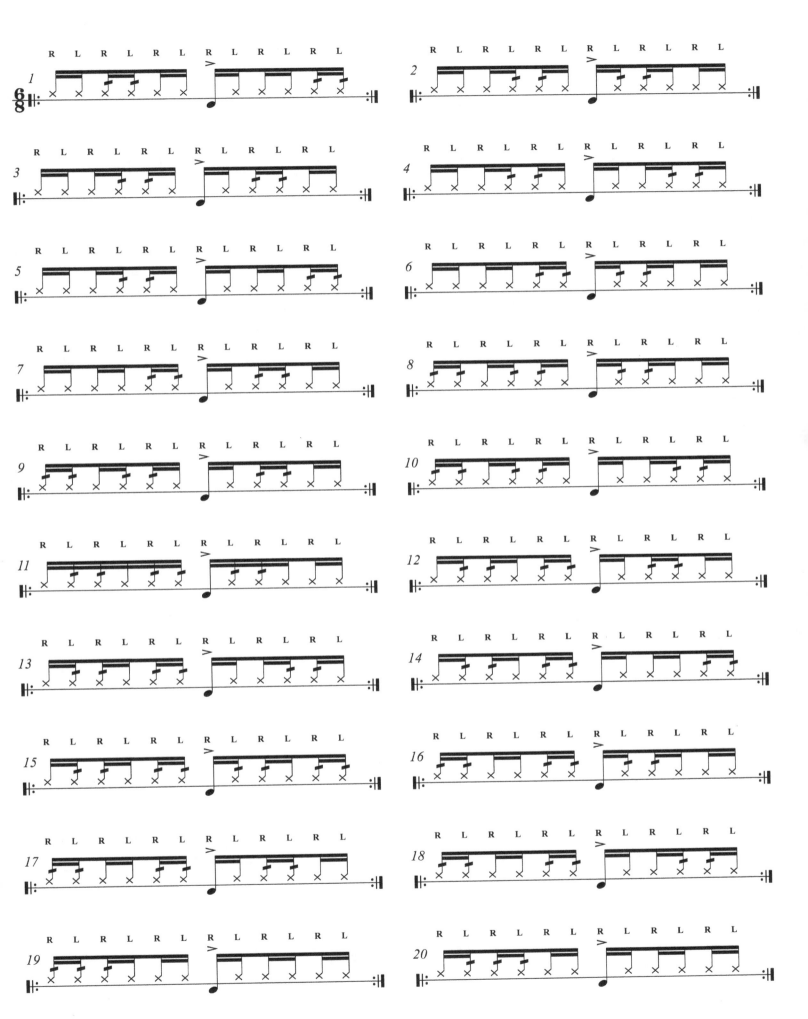

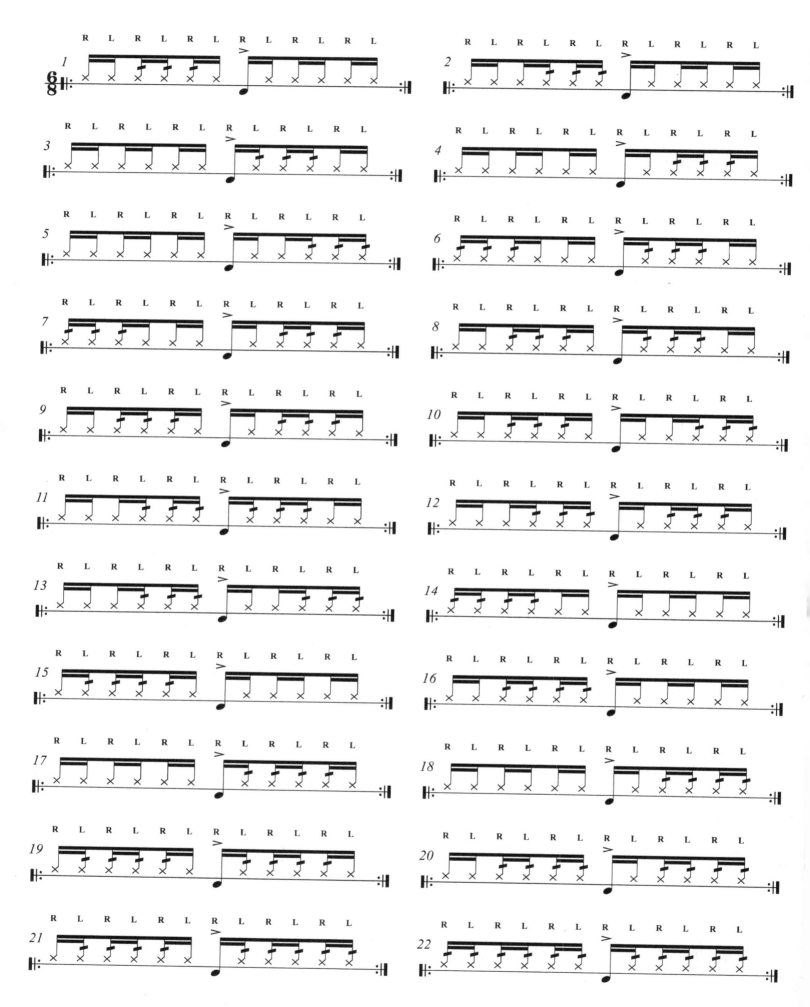

108

VARIATIONS ON THE HI-HAT ROCK BEAT
WITH 16th NOTE TRIPLETS IN 2/4 TIME

Precede each exercise with two bars of the standard rock beat on hi-hat with alternating hands.

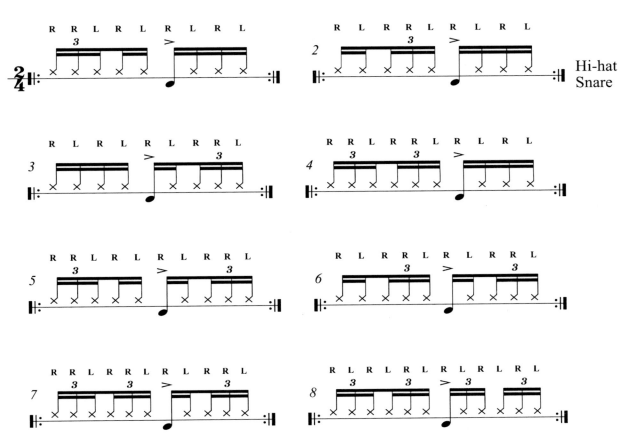

VARIATIONS WITH QUINTUPLETS

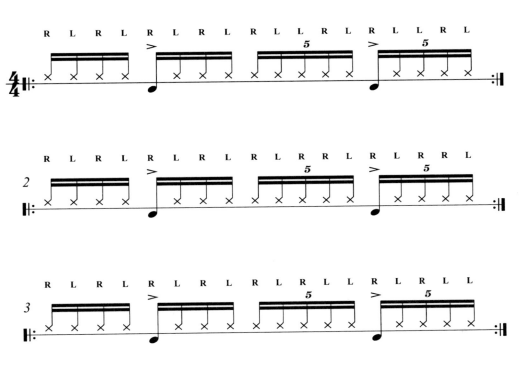

OTHER BOOKS BY JOEL ROTHMAN

Four-Way Independence
For Rock Drumming

Mini-Monster Book Of Rock Drumming

Son Of The Mini Monster
For Rock Drumming

Rock
With Hand-Foot Drum Breaks

Rock Breaks Around The Drums

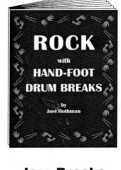

Reading, Rudiments and Rock Drumming

The Bible Of Linear Drumming
(For All True Believers)

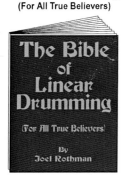

The Fantastic Jazz Drum Book

Drumming Outside The Box
For Rock & Jazz

Jazz Breaks In A Nutshell

Linear Jazz Drumming

Easy Drum Solos
For Jazz Coordination

Reading, Rudiments, & Marching Cadences

Blood, Sweat & Rudiments

Basic Drum Technique And Beyond

Sticking Patterns
For All Drummers

Rudiments Around The Drums

Rudiment Etudes
For Snare Drum

45 Minutes, 33 Seconds
Concerto For Drum Set

Big Band Drum Charts

Hardest Drum Book Ever Written

Orchestral Snare Drumming

Rolls, Rolls, Rolls

Crazy Mixed-Up Meters

Mini-Monster Book Rock Drumming
ISBN 978-1-617-27013-0

JR Publications, LLC
c/o Charles Dumont & Son, Inc. 1085 Dumont Drive, Voorhees, NJ 08043 • 1-800-257-8283
If you teach drums e-mail: info@joelrothman.com
View all of Joel's books at: www.joelrothman.com